A LEGACY OF LEARNING

A LEGACY OF LEARNING

Your Stake in Standards and New Kinds of Public Schools

David T. Kearns *and* James Harvey

BROOKINGS INSTITUTION PRESS
Washington, D.C.

Copyright © 2000

THE BROOKINGS INSTITUTION
1775 Massachusetts Avenue, N.W., Washington, D.C. 20036
www.brook.edu

Library of Congress Cataloging-in-Publication data

Kearns, David T.
  A legacy of learning : your stake in standards and new kinds of public schools / David T. Kearns and James Harvey.
      p.   cm.
  Includes bibliographical references and index.
    ISBN 0-8157-4894-9 (alk. paper)
    1. Educational change—United States. 2. Public schools—United States—Evaluation. 3. Education—Standards—United States. I. Harvey, James, 1944- II. Title.
  LA217.2 K43 2000   99-050467
  371.01'0973—dc21   CIP

9 8 7 6 5 4 3 2 1

The paper used in this publication meets minimum requirements of the American National Standard for Information Sciences—Permanence of Paper for Printed Library Materials: ANSI Z39.48-1984.

Typeset in Minion

Composition by Linda C. Humphrey

Printed by R. R. Donnelly & Sons
Harrisonburg, Virginia

Contents

Foreword

I'VE KNOWN DAVID KEARNS for many years. We first met when I was vice president under Ronald Reagan and he was chairman of the Xerox Corporation, and we quickly built a rapport that lasts to this day. I respected his accomplishments as Xerox chairman, and I came to admire the intensity and enthusiasm he displayed for transforming American schools.

When he stepped down from Xerox in late 1990, we recruited him as deputy secretary of education. He helped my administration develop an ambitious education agenda— one that supported the national education goals with more parental options, local school autonomy, and greater accountability. These ideas are alive and well today, and I'm proud of this education legacy.

I'm a big believer in the core message of this book: Education is not simply a domestic priority, it just may be *the* domestic priority. Despite our economic success, the world remains a dangerous place and a very competitive one. We cannot succeed in this environment without a system of schooling that provides all our young people, not just a few, with the basic education they need to make informed decisions, improve their communities, understand their responsibilities as parents and neighbors, and earn their way in the world. We need an entire populace educated to "think for a living."

In several ways this book provides some very good answers to many of the often-asked questions on education. It offers examples of things that work, like New American Schools. It asks all of us to get involved. It explains why change in our education system is so tough. David Kearns has always believed our country needs better schools. We need schools that are world class. We need new kinds of schools, constructed around new concepts of what a "public school" can be. This book explains why these ideas are so important, in language all of us can understand. It offers solutions, not just problems. It asks each of us to shed our complacency, and, most important, it insists that all of us together take the steps needed to protect our children's educational future—and our country's.

GEORGE BUSH
Houston, Texas

Acknowledgments

A BOOK LIKE THIS could never have been developed
without the advice, cooperation, assistance, and patience
of dozens of people. We want to acknowledge their help
here.

Without Shirley Kearns's encouragement throughout
the process, this volume would never have seen the light
of day. Shirley was an early fan for a book that would cap-
ture some of the lessons of David's experiences. She
proved to be a tireless and inexhaustible supporter as we
moved forward.

Craig Pattee brought the two of us together and was a
solid source of counsel throughout our struggles with the
book. He worried about the process, thought through next
steps, and chimed in with invaluable suggestions on text
and context. We also want to acknowledge the contributions of Barbara Martz, a public affairs specialist in New
York. Barbara helped us understand how to frame our
message for different audiences and put us in touch with
several sources of valuable help.

In developing the text, five members of David's personal
staff were steadfast in their enthusiasm. And at different

stages, Maryann Hoffman, Jeff Lindley, Matthew Barnes, Josh Bourne, and Ben Wallerstein provided essential support.

We are particularly grateful to several people who put up with our questions and inquiries. All of them educated us for the better, sometimes without being aware of it. First, we want to mention Lamar Alexander, formerly governor of Tennessee and U.S. secretary of education; John Anderson, president of New American Schools; Edward Bales from Motorola; Stacey Boyd, founding director of the Academy of the Pacific Rim, Hyde Park, Massachusetts; Ben Canada, Portland, Oregon, school superintendent; Raymon Cortines, former chancellor of New York City public schools; Denis Doyle, the Hudson Institute; Wade Dyke, David's former colleague in the Department of Education, now with Cambridge Academies; Checker Finn, the Hudson Institute; Howard Fuller, head of the Institute for the Transformation of Learning at Marquette University and former Milwaukee school superintendent; Robert Galvin, former chairman and CEO of the Motorola Company; Milton Goldberg, vice president of the National Alliance of Business; Scott Hamilton, former director of the Massachusetts charter school program; Paul T. Hill, the Daniel J. Evans School of Public Affairs at the University of Washington; and Hazel Hobbs, a former public elementary school principal and retired headmistress of the Pear Tree Point School in Darien, Connecticut.

We also acknowledge what we learned from Gerry House, superintendent in Memphis, Tennessee; John Immerwahr of the Public Agenda Foundation; Jack Jennings, former majority counsel to the Education and Labor Committee in the U.S. House of Representatives; S. Jefferson Kennard III, formerly a colleague of David's at Xerox; Diana Lam, former superintendent in San Antonio, now leading the schools in Providence, Rhode Island; Bruno Manno of the Hudson Institute; Deborah Meier of Boston's Pilot School Project; Donald E. Petersen, former chairman and CEO of Ford Motor Company; Frank Pipp, recently retired from Xerox; William Raspberry, columnist, the *Washington Post*; Diane Ravitch, the Brookings Institution and New York University; Jack Rennie, president of Pacer, Inc., in Massachusetts; Roy Romer, chairman of the Democratic National Committee and former governor of Colorado;

Ted Sizer, former director of the Coalition for Essential Schools; Tim Smucker, CEO of the Smucker Company; Susan Traiman from the Business Roundtable; Bill Wigginhorn of Motorola University; and Saul Yanofsky, school superintendent, White Plains, New York.

Throughout the development of this book, James Harvey enjoyed access to some of the latest thinking about school reform through his attendance at the meetings of the Danforth Foundation's Forum for the American School Superintendent. This provided the two of us with a fascinating window into school administration for which we are grateful. Harvey wants to acknowledge in particular the debt he owes to his colleagues on the Forum's steering committee—Bob Koff, senior vice president of the Danforth Foundation; Richard Wallace, former Pittsburgh school superintendent; Bertha Pendleton, former superintendent in San Diego; Nelda Cambron-McCabe of Miami University, Oxford, Ohio; Marquette's Howard Fuller; and Vern Cunningham, professor emeritus at Ohio State University. The forum, its members, and its steering committee provided an ongoing seminar on American schools that helped shape this book in many ways.

Several people saved us from ourselves by acting as "critical friends" who reviewed the book in manuscript form: Shirley Kearns; Anne Paxton, Jim Harvey's wife; John Anderson; Denis Doyle; Paul Hill; Anna C. Puglia, assistant principal of Branford High School in Branford, Connecticut; Diane Ravitch; Ted Sizer; and Al Viebranz, recently retired from GTE. Harvey's Washington, D.C., colleagues, Peter Slavin and Randall Mawer, also offered helpful suggestions about the book's very early ideas.

We want to express our deep appreciation to Philip Spitzer, our agent. Philip educated us in the challenges of producing a book, introduced us to the complexities of the modern publishing industry, and never flagged in his interest in seeing our book through to completion.

Finally, we thank our editor at Brookings, Marty Gottron, who refused to tolerate vagueness or imprecision from either of us.

To all of these friends and colleagues, we offer our sincere thanks. We are grateful for the insights they provided and trust we have not done violence to their ideas. Although we do not pretend that all of them share the views expressed here, whatever merit the book possesses belongs at least in equal measure to them. The two of us, of course, take responsibility for any mistakes.

DAVID T. KEARNS

JAMES HARVEY

A LEGACY OF LEARNING

Introduction

FOR EIGHTEEN MONTHS, starting early in 1991, the two of us worked on one of the most exhilarating ventures in the history of American schools. We cannot say that we worked together on it, because we knew each other only by reputation and ran into each other just once. But we shared a common vision. The venture was the establishment of the New American Schools (NAS) Development Corporation. NAS was a core element in "America 2000," an effort spearheaded by Secretary of Education Lamar Alexander to reinvigorate American communities and reinvent American schools. The NAS vision, which developed into the most significant privately funded reform effort ever mounted in American education, involved putting an end to cookie-cutter education in the United States by developing exciting new ideas about what schools might look like and innovative new models of what schools could be.

America 2000 and NAS were Lamar Alexander's answer to a question President George Bush posed to a group of university presidents in 1989, when Alexander was president of the University of Tennessee. "If we have the best universities in the world," Bush asked "why can't we have the best schools?"[1] Like most good questions, it led to some pretty good answers. These included the development of the national education goals by President Bush and the governors of fifty states; America 2000, a Bush legislative program, which Congress refused to enact; and the Clinton administration's Goals 2000, which Congress passed grudgingly in 1994 after watering them down.[2]

Although the two of us worked together in establishing the New American Schools Development Corporation, we played very different roles. David Kearns provided the leadership to establish NAS as a nonprofit corporation funded entirely by private and philanthropic dollars. James Harvey helped NAS flush the most promising educational ideas into the open and select the best of them for support. Kearns, fresh from the chairmanship of Xerox, was the man who grasped the big picture, understood the broader environment, and knew what it meant to assemble a small team capable of transforming a large organization. Harvey, a successful consultant since 1983, when he helped the National Commission on Excellence in Education produce the landmark report *A Nation at Risk,* was the writer who developed the NAS prospectus calling for "a new kind of American school."

The NAS prospectus, addressed to "dreamers and doers from all walks of life" and inviting "all who care about the nation's education future to become architects of a new generation of American schools," was hailed enthusiastically by major elements of the education community.[3] NAS had planned to hold one "design conference" on the prospectus; it was thought that 200 to 300 experts might be interested in offering advice and that 80 to 100 proposals might be received. It quickly became clear that public interest was enormous. NAS found itself holding three conferences—two in the Washington area and a third in Los Angeles—with several thousand people at each and with one of them televised and distributed via satellite and cable. On Valentine's Day, 1992, the close of the competition, 687 proposals were in NAS's mailbags.[4]

Our story is not so much about NAS as it is about the difficulty of transforming American schools. Although NAS figures prominently in this drama, the play could be written with a completely different set of characters. But we learned enough from watching it and other reform efforts that we think many people can benefit from our experience. Our objective, therefore, is threefold.

First, we want again to make the case for radical (that is to say deeply rooted) public school reform. No more tinkering around the margins. We describe in detail what is wrong with the schools we have today and why they are so hard to change. Despite the promises of more than a decade of reform, energy is being wasted as the education establishment fine-tunes failure. Since the landmark report, *A Nation at Risk,* woke Americans to the startling failures of the education system in 1983, student performance has remained essentially flat. Rather than respond with the alarm that is called for, the education establishment has shrugged its shoulders, middle-class parents have fled to private schools, and community leaders have thrown up their hands.

Then we want to share our thoughts on the broader question of how to transform American schools. Too many educators have just ignored their critics, shrugging off complaints like a duck shedding water. Parents and their children need more options, more alternatives, and more choice. Without them, neither the New American School designs nor dozens of other promising efforts can thrive. The truth is that completely new strategies are needed to reinvent American schools. American society will never change the schools it has as long as it begins by asking permission from the people who now manage them. For public schools no longer belong to the public, but to the professionals in them. It is time the public took them back.

Americans need to put first things first. Learning is what schools are primarily about. Both of us want children to develop physically, emotionally, and socially—and to feel good about themselves, too. Schools have a role to play in all that. But their most important role is helping students develop intellectually. It is time for everyone to take standards and student achievement seriously.

Finally, we try to explain how communities, indeed, the larger culture and the entire society, need to change their ways. Too many Americans are in denial about just how serious the problem is and how they have contributed to it. As intimidating as the first two tasks were to both of us at the outset, they turned out to be the easiest of the three assignments we set ourselves. The third and most difficult was the effort to provide American parents and their fellow citizens with an action agenda to move reform along.

In many ways, American society does not encourage learning or even value it very much. Parents are often busier worrying about their children's popularity than their learning when they insist that they want their kids to be "well rounded." It is time to change all of this. It is time the public and major American institutions understood that public education is a public responsibility shared by everyone in our society.

We want to share what we have learned because we are convinced there are lessons to be gleaned as the effort to improve American schools continues. And we are also telling this story because crucial issues confront Americans today. Despite the nation's current prosperity, its competitiveness in a global economy remains a long-term concern. Equally serious, the development of a two-track economy within the United States threatens to sabotage the nation's future. The American experiment cannot succeed if it grows along two distinct tracks, one offering satisfying work, opportunity, and fulfillment to the well-educated, the other consigning the poorly educated to a life of unskilled labor, hardship, and broken promises. If we adults are to sustain the nation economically for our children and if we are to pass on to them the quality of life and values we hold dear, our schools must be reinvented and revitalized.

Writing this book was a learning experience for the two of us. We found it very helpful to sit down and examine our own biases and preferences against the history of school reform. It turns out that Owen "Brad" Butler, a former president of Procter & Gamble, was correct. One of Brad's favorite sayings was, "The problem isn't always what we don't know. More often, it's what we know that just ain't so." As we worked on this book we found a lot of things we thought we knew that just "ain't so."

There are three distinct education problems in the United States today. One is what the two of us think of as misplaced smugness and complacency about the quality of suburban schools. They look pretty good compared with their urban and rural counterparts. But they are a pale imitation of a real school compared with schools abroad.

Then there are the education problems of rural America. These communities have a lot of difficulties, including even more severe achievement difficulties than those exhibited in suburbia. And they also have major financial headaches associated with the poverty of their communities and their inability to finance the education improvements they need.

Third, American urban education is a national disgrace. Despite large expenditures on big-city schools, nothing seems to work. These communities and their schools are prisoners of poverty. They are hostages to despair. But that does not have to be the case. Our society can give young people in these communities hope for the future. The road out of poverty and despair leads through the schoolhouse door. The children of the poor must be given the same kinds of education options and choices that the children of affluence take for granted. At root, that is the promise that lies at the heart of the proposals in this book.

Chapter 1 is an overview of our entire argument. Because some stalwarts in the education establishment insist that the crisis in education is imaginary. Chapter 2 examines national and international data to illustrate how well American schools are doing. Chapter 3 describes the decent impulses that underlie the development of the American common school and how they went astray, leading to the situation we describe in chapter 4 of institutional inertia and gridlock paralyzing reform efforts.

The next four chapters start to pull together the elements that will be required to turn around a system involving about 122,000 public and private schools and more than 55 million students. Leaving our children a legacy of learning will require a lot of work. Chapter 5 examines how other huge institutions, including government institutions and several Fortune 100 companies, have dealt successfully with their own quality problems. Chapter 6 examines how those lessons apply to American schools. In chapters 7 and 8 we turn our attention to promising models of reform, beginning with the great hopes we have for the whole-school reform efforts of New American Schools and continuing with descriptions of several other significant reform thrusts.

The final chapters develop our reform agenda. In chapter 9 we talk about the politics of reform, arguing that a more coherent system is needed, one in which innovation and parental choice are taken for granted. Chapter 10 takes up the complicated issues of systemic reform, pointing to the importance of the national education goals as the North Star of the effort, defining governmental roles, and calling, among other things, for uniform standards, better assessments, and improved teacher training. Chapter 11 calls for hardwiring innovation into the system in two ways. First, we recommend near universal adoption of whole-school reform models at the elementary level. Second, we call for supporting secondary education by creating renewable, innovative schools through contracts with eligible nonprofit agencies. American society needs a new kind of public school system, one that encourages across-the-board innovation and parental choice. Chapter 12 lays out what the public must do to help create this reform agenda. Analysts and public officials can only do so much. Without public support, the proposals described here—and other reform proposals as well—inevitably will wither and die.

The two of us have collaborated to tell this story. In truth, you will be hearing an account from two perspectives, combining whatever knowledge, insight, and experience we have. For clarity, however, we use only one voice. David Kearns is the narrator.

CHAPTER ONE

We Need
to Change

WHAT IS WRONG WITH the American education system? Why can't we fix our schools? How did the United States wind up with high school dropout rates of 25 percent *and* graduates who can barely read and write? Who is responsible for the fiasco that sees up to 60 percent of new teachers failing basic tests of reading and writing? In the face of shockingly poor performance by American students on nationwide and international tests, what explains the "Lake Wobegon" effect, the phenomenon of state and local educators reporting that America's children are all above average? Why does the United States spend twice as much on education as the international average and end up at the bottom of the barrel in global comparisons of student achievement? What happened to cause American preeminence in high school completion rates to slip so that the United States now trails twenty-two other industrialized nations? What can be done about all this?[1]

Those are the issues I set out to examine in this book. After a three-year investigation, I am not at all convinced that conventional educators have the answers. Often they are not even asking the right questions. For the most part their reform prescriptions simply fine-tune failure. Interest group politics define what is possible because public schools are no longer "the public's schools" but creatures of the professionals who manage them. Despite worshiping at the altar of "local control," communities all across the United States have managed to create cookie-cutter schools while sidestepping the transparent need for common expectations and standards about what students should know and be able to do. Above all, we Americans have met the enemy and it is us: All of us support change as long as someone else changes.

Effective school reform is not rocket science. Educators and policymakers should not act as if most Americans cannot follow this discussion or understand what is required. Education reform needs to get back on track. Our children deserve a world-class education. Citizens across the nation need to demand an end to public school systems that provide a one-size-fits-all education and assign children to schools depending on where they live. The nation needs a new definition of what a public school is, as well as a much more open and democratic schooling system that provides real choices to meet the diverse interests of American students. Society needs public schools that truly belong to the public because citizens know them, understand them, and support them.

Above all, we Americans need to leave behind a legacy of learning for our children. It should take the form of high standards and expectations for student performance. It should include new kinds of public schools that are capable of continual self-renewal and confident enough of their value to offer abundant options to American students and families.

To me nothing is more important to the American future than the quality of the schools. Educational performance is the fundamental issue lying at the core of every problem our society faces—economic performance, domestic tranquillity, international competitiveness, racial harmony, and the growing gap between rich and poor in America. No matter how you circle around these issues, all of them sooner or later come back to the schools.

This country cannot work unless its schools do. That is my fundamental conviction. It cannot work economically, it will not work socially, and it will not be able to function as a democracy. The issue is at once that simple, that straightforward, that direct—and that important.

Education and Competitiveness: The Economic Equation

A strong nation depends on a strong education system. Education and economic competitiveness are two sides of the same coin. It is really that simple.

I first came to the education issue in the 1970s. And I came to it not as a starry-eyed idealist, but as a businessman. I had become convinced that the competitive success of corporations (and nations) depended increasingly on the quality of their human resources. My initial interest was really nothing more than that. Manufacturers were continually trying to improve processes and the quality of the raw materials that go into their products. It had become clear to me that the human element in the design and production process could be improved too.

Our competitors in the Pacific Rim understand that. The Japanese, for example, seemed to me to view universal education as key to international competitiveness, influence on the world stage, national unity, cultural cohesion, and personal development. Here in the United States, parental interest in schools, when it exists at all, is often much more pedestrian: Are my children popular? Do they have friends? Do they seem to be happy and doing well? How good is the football team? Small wonder that Japanese students run circles around American students on international achievement tests.

According to American scholars who have studied these matters in depth, the success of Japanese schools (and for that matter Chinese schools, on the mainland or on Taiwan) is rooted deep in Asian culture. For example, Harold Stevenson of the University of Michigan and James Stigler of the University of California, Los Angeles, both social scientists, report distinct differences in the cultural contexts in which American, Japanese, and Chinese schools find themselves.[2] Japanese and Chinese schools are able to insist on higher achievement because the home and the community support high standards, hard work, and respect for teachers.

Struggling to understand the competitive pressures toppling one American industrial giant after another, I went to Japan perhaps twenty-five times or more during my time at Xerox. The company had a joint venture in Japan, Fuji Xerox. In my conversations with Tony Kobayashi, chief executive officer of Fuji Xerox, and Jeff Kennard, a Xerox representative who helped manage relations with our Japanese business ally, I learned a lot about Japanese society and Japanese schools. These lessons confirmed expert opinion.

According to Tony and Jeff, Japanese education continues to be influenced by Confucian ethics of respect for learning, discipline, diligence, and responsibility. Above all, they told me, the Japanese have a respect for teachers that borders on reverence. Jeff, in fact, believed that the challenge to the United States "comes primarily from the Japanese classroom, not the factory."[3] In his view, the literate, competent, and diligent workers with whom American workers are competing were produced first and foremost by Japanese schools. Education equals competitiveness; that is the basic equation.

Despite the disastrous performance of the Japanese economy in the last half of the 1990s, the basic equation still holds. Japan rose from the ashes of World War II by taking American statements about education standards and student performance seriously and harnessing them to Confucian principles. Like a phoenix, Japan will emerge intact again from today's economic ashes. We Americans should take our own educational ideals as seriously as do our friends in the Land of the Rising Sun.

I think Tony and Jeff had it just about right. The Japanese culture, the entire society, is almost obsessively committed to children and education. There is even a sort of national consensus on what the ideal Japanese child should look like. No such consensus exists in the United States, and most people, including myself, would not want such a thing. Americans value individual differences too much for that. But partly because American society values individuality, there is no clear consensus about what young people should know and be able to do when they complete high school.

Most parents are like my wife Shirley and me: they want schools to help prepare their children for life. At its most obvious, that means preparing them for the world of work. For most people, work is part of the rhythm of life. But life encompasses much more than earning a living. Parents, and indeed the larger society, also want their children to become good parents. They want their children to understand what it means to be part of a neighborhood and to contribute to their communities, often in leadership positions. They want their children to grow up to be citizens with an active interest in the great events of the day. And they want people who know how to use, enjoy, and profit from the leisure that is the fruit of their work.

In many ways what society wants is quite simple. Schools should help produce adults who can discharge all of the obligations that go with earning a living, being a parent, living in a community, and being a member of a democratic society. Pretty simple—and simultaneously pretty complex. The difficulty is that our schools are not producing these kinds of graduates.

These tasks are much more formidable today than they were just a generation ago. Every careful observer of contemporary life believes that American society has undergone dramatic social and economic transformations in recent decades. However good or bad today's schools are judged relative to those of the past, they are unlikely to be good enough to meet societal and individual expectations for the future.

The Jobs Connection

Ed Bales, who retired in 1997 after ten years with the Motorola Company's training arm, Motorola University, likes to point out that as the United States moved from an agrarian society in the nineteenth century to an industrial one in the twentieth, everything about the economy changed. Not only did the nation move from agriculture to manufacturing, but the tools, resources, and ways of organizing people for work were transformed as well. A similar upheaval is taking place in workers' lives today as the nation moves into the information age, he says.[4]

The dominant technology of the agricultural era was the plow, notes Bales. The product was food, developed with strategic resources of land and animal energy. As industrial needs came to predominate, heavy equipment and machinery became the major technologies, manufactured goods became the product, and strategic resources of capital and fossil fuels displaced land and the brute power of men and animals. As the world moves into the information age, the computer is becoming the essential tool, information is the critical product, and human knowledge and the human mind are the major strategic resources as well as the greatest source of economic energy.

How have American schools responded to all of this? Not terribly well. Everyone can point to an exception here and there, but by and large the schools today are the same ones that were created in the agrarian past. Even the school calendar in use today was designed originally with farm needs in mind and has been expanded only grudgingly ever since.[5] Everything else has changed dramatically, but schools have hardly changed at all.

The big changes in the larger society are accompanied by significant dislocations, often painful and traumatic. Although service employment has partially compensated for the loss of manufacturing jobs in the United States (and absorbed huge numbers of women into the labor force), it seldom pays as well as manufacturing. Middle-class American households have had to rely on two incomes to sustain their living standards. The importance of child care and of schools as places for socializing the young have begun to become more apparent.

Standards everywhere today are higher. It is hard to find a typewriter in an office; they have been replaced by computers. Today's mechanics do not guess at what is wrong with an engine, they diagnose it with onboard electronic systems. Technology in industries from printing to automaking turns around every two to three years. The half-life of today's engineering graduates is said to be about five years; then they have to retool themselves. Roy Romer, who was governor of Colorado when I spoke with him and is now chairman of the Democratic National Committee, told me he likes to use a pole-vaulting analogy to get the message across. "Americans are still trying to vault a fifteen-foot bar with bamboo poles out of the 1950s while the rest of the world is clearing nineteen feet easily with fiberglass," Romer says.[6]

In his writings throughout the 1990s, Peter Drucker makes several vital points about the future of the U.S. and world economy and education. He asserts that the era of stable and highly paid blue-collar jobs necessitating only minimal levels of education is over, that stable industrial firms are almost a thing of the past, and that people will be forced to choose between lower-paid service jobs and relatively better-paying "knowledge worker jobs."[7]

As Drucker points out, knowledge workers, by definition, have to master specialized skills. They also have to be extremely adaptable. They seldom work in assembly lines, and the organizations that employ them are themselves lean and adaptable. Thus, the new generation of knowledge workers will have to shape their own skills and work to the current needs of an unpredictable economy. They will also have to manage their own careers, understanding the environment in which they work well enough to know when to develop new skills, when to leave one job for another, and when to start something new on their own.

I find Drucker's analysis compelling. Its education implications are sobering. Obviously, all Americans will need very high levels of skills. But they will also have to develop the capacity to analyze their own situations and to understand how they fit into larger systems. They must have the breadth of knowledge and skills, including adaptable mathematical, verbal, and foreign language skills, that our society currently strives to inculcate only in our most able liberal arts graduates.

I can already hear the naysayers. Some of them are probably thinking right now: "So what? If education and economic competitiveness are two sides of the same coin and the schools are as bad as Kearns says they are, how come the U.S. economy is roaring ahead and Japan is suffering through its worst recession since World War II? So what if the Japanese and Koreans and the French and the Germans beat us on international comparisons? They have all got double-digit inflation and lots of their people can't find work. Get a life." Others are likely to be saying. "Right. American companies have already made miraculous competitive recoveries with the very work force produced by the schools he is criticizing. If the schools are so bad, how did these companies pull off that feat?"

Fair enough. Good observations all, but they miss the point: education and competitiveness are two sides of the same coin. America's economic success is made possible not only by the public schools, but also by the American system of higher education. The United States leads the world in the proportion of adults with a bachelor's degree.[8] The work force on which the economy and companies depend is made up increasingly of the college educated. In many ways, the nation's competitive rebound has been driven by American higher education, a system that in international circles is almost universally described as the "envy of the world."

A 1996 report from the Business–Higher Education Forum (B–HEF) nicely demonstrated the extent to which major corporations rely on college-educated personnel. Under the leadership of Harold "Red" Poling, newly retired from his position as chairman and CEO of Ford Motor Company, B–HEF set out to examine the work readiness of college graduates. One part of that investigation involved examining nine large American companies, ranging from McDonald's and Federal Express in the services area, to Chase Manhattan in banking, and Xerox and Ford Motor Company in manufacturing and high technology. Poling wanted to know several things, including how much money companies spent on training new hires from the college ranks. He also wanted to know how many people were hired each year at each company and what proportion of them were college graduates. The findings, for the eight companies providing complete data, are displayed in table 1-1.

What becomes immediately apparent from the table is that most of these companies are hiring large numbers and proportions of college graduates. The exception is McDonald's, which provides low-technology services, where college graduates make up less than 4 percent of new hires. Federal Express, more high-tech than McDonald's but still service-oriented, and Ford Motor Company, one of the great manufacturing enterprises in the world, both report that about one-fourth of their new hires are college grads. With the exception of AT&T (where college graduates make up 35 percent of new hires), everyone else—whether in banking (Chase Manhattan), publishing (Hallmark Cards), professional services (Arthur Andersen), or manufacturing and high technology (Xerox)—reports that about half or more of new workers had college degrees. And I would guess that many of the new hires that did not have college degrees had one or more years of college work under their belt.

So my basic position is intact. Yet this happy state of affairs comes at considerable economic cost. According to the most recent evidence, 78 percent of higher education institutions offer remedial courses in reading, writing, and mathematics.[9] Sound surprising? How about this: 29 percent of all first-time freshmen enroll in at least one of these courses each fall.[10] When one considers that this 29 percent of first-year students is from that half of high school graduates who go on to college, the implications are truly staggering.

We Americans have created a two-step system to provide the work force we need. Society is paying twice to develop fundamental skills,

TABLE 1-1
Overview of Eight Corporations

Name	Type of business	U.S. employees	Annual new hires	College hires	As percent of new hires
AT&T	Telecommunications	217,298	8,630	~3,000	35
Arthur Andersen	Professional services	32,358	8,917	7,237	81
Chase Manhattan	Finance	26,913	7,030	3,348	48
Federal Express	Transportation	96,945	22,463	5,221	23
Ford Motor Company	Manufacturing	149,921	11,070	2,723	25
Hallmark	Publication, retail sales	12,684	328	223	68
McDonald's	Restaurants	426,053	549,747	20,115	3.6
Xerox	Manufacturing	47,176	2,053	979	48

Source: Business–Higher Education Forum, *Higher Education and Work Readiness: The View from the Corporation* (Washington, D.C.: 1995).

first in public schools and, when that does not work, in institutions of higher education. The schools should get it right the first time.

But this issue is about more than jobs. Buried in table 1-1 is a very troubling set of numbers for people who care about economic equity. McDonald's appears to be hiring many more people than other major companies. It is also hiring many more high school graduates and dropouts than most other major corporations. In fact, McDonald's appears to be hiring more people on an annual basis than its total domestic employment base. To the extent that McDonald's represents the fast-food industry, these statistics indicate the development of a two-track economy in the United States. On one track are relatively stable, high-paying jobs with a future available to the well-educated at places such as Xerox and Ford Motor Company. On the other track are low-paying jobs in the low-tech service sector with very little future and extremely high turnover. The United States as a functioning democracy cannot stand by and consign one segment of its young people to that kind of future.

A Functioning Democracy

The education issue is about much more than jobs. It runs to the very core of society. Commentaries in recent years from sources as diverse as the conservative analyst Kevin Phillips and the Congressional Budget Office (CBO) underscore a steady and startling growth in income inequality in the United States.[11] According to the CBO, for example, the top fifth of households earns 50 percent of national earnings, while the bottom two-fifths account for only 14 percent. In actual dollars the average income of the top 20 percent of American households was $89,000 in 1990, and the bottom 20 percent had to get by on less than one-tenth of that amount, $8,202 annually.

The social implications of growing poverty are formidable. The dramatic reduction in the share of annual earnings for the bottom fifth undoubtedly increases social anger and helps elevate crime rates. Meanwhile, at the very time that low-income households find the wolf at the door and middle-income households often find themselves with less to spend even with two wage-earners hard at work, the wealthy worry about crime and complain about the costs of supporting community services.

I witnessed the effects of much of this first-hand in the spring of 1992, when President Bush asked me to coordinate the federal response to the Los Angeles riots that followed the acquittal of the policemen involved in the filmed beating of Rodney King. I asked community leaders how local residents and gang members justified torching property and businesses in their own neighborhoods. The question provoked an outpouring of anger and frustration describing young men and women with no hope for the future. Their families had been on welfare for generations. They had no sense of ownership in society; indeed, they gave off an overpowering sense of the tragic futility of their lives.

Yet, even the gang members I spoke with understood that schools were important to the neighborhood. Amidst the carnage of these riots, schools lay relatively untouched. Even the most disenchanted citizens of south central Los Angeles understood the importance of fixing schools. Simply put, schools are a fundamental solution to many of the problems in this society.

Although the social consequences of poverty may be debated, there is little controversy about the connection to education. To be poorly educated is to run a substantial and growing risk of being poor throughout life. At the same time, to be well educated is to have the world by the tail. High school graduates enjoy incomes 50 percent higher than dropouts; college graduates are even further ahead, with incomes at least 75 percent higher, on average, than high school graduates.

Socio-Demographic Change

Meanwhile, the face of America is changing. Although most American families with children continue in the Norman Rockwell image (about seven out of ten American children live with two parents), demographers say that reality is changing:

— Many children are now born out of wedlock; although most are white children, the number includes about two-thirds of all African American children, nearly half of whom live in poverty.[12]

— Hispanic and Asian Americans will account for 61 percent of the growth in American population between 1995 and 2025.

— Once so-called "minority" youngsters now constitute growing proportions of school populations and in the nation's largest state, California, already constitute a majority.[13]

— By the year 2005 the majority of students in American public schools will be nonwhite.[14]

— By the year 2015 the number of Hispanic Americans will equal the number of African Americans.[15]

— Half of all children and youth will be members of minority groups by 2025, and half of the entire population will be minority by 2050.[16]

— About 75 percent of American women between the ages of twenty-five and sixty-five, the women formerly engaged in child rearing and child care, are today employed outside the home.[17]

— Huge absolute numbers of immigrant students do not speak English as a first language, and many of their parents do not speak English at all.

The United States has become such an ethnic stew that Americans hardly know if they are fish or fowl anymore. As Gerald Seib described the United States recently in the *Wall Street Journal:*

Today, Muslims outnumber Episcopalians. Three out of four Americans, some 192.5 million, are whites, but the population also includes 32.5 million African Americans, almost 26 million Hispanics, and nine million Asian Americans. The idea of all those Americans identifying themselves as members of some subset, rather than parts of the whole, is frightening. Americans will need unifying institutions that work.[18]

Schools are one of the few unifying institutions in our communities. Part of being a good citizen is participating in our democracy. That requires making decisions about often complex issues, frequently on very short notice. Good citizens have to be able to interpret what they see on television news; they have to be able to read and understand a newspaper. Without a solid education, it is hard to contribute fully in a vibrant democracy.

Our Schools Are Not Working

In short, for the country to function, its schools must work well. They must work better than they have ever worked before. Yet, these vital institutions are not now working well enough. As this book documents:

—The longer today's American students go to school, the more poorly they perform compared with American students of a generation ago.

—Equally distressing, the longer children stay in school, the poorer their performance is compared with that of their peers abroad.

—Functional illiteracy among recent graduates is startlingly high, running up to about 40 percent in minority communities.

—Dropout rates from American secondary schools are scandalously high, averaging about 25 percent overall.

—We have accomplished a remarkable double: not only do about one-quarter of our young people drop out of secondary school, but 25 percent or more of those who graduate cannot meet today's demands for reading and writing.

The news, thank God, is not all unalloyed pessimism. The good news is that in some areas the system seems to be doing reasonably well. Pockets of excellence can be found in promising new models such as those being underwritten by New American Schools, the venture I helped establish during the Bush presidency and which Secretary of Education Richard Riley of the Clinton administration continues to support.

Student achievement in the elementary grades is also excellent. According to the latest 1996 and 1997 reports, American fourth graders rank second in the world in reading; stand either second or third in science, depending on how one reads the results; and are well above average in mathematics.[19] These successes should be celebrated—not simply because fairness requires it, but because these results are genuinely encouraging. We should be able to build on them.

At the secondary level, however, U.S. students are just about last in the world in mathematics and science achievement. And the most recent domestic analysis from the National Assessment of Educational Progress (NAEP) indicates that only two-thirds of high school graduates appear to have mastered the essentials they need in areas such as mathematics and science.

Can the Country Succeed?

The question is whether we Americans will continue to accept this kind of performance. Can our country succeed if the longer its students remain in school the more their performance deteriorates? Can we stand by and watch a system transform demonstrably superior performance in literacy and science in the early years into demonstrable failure by twelfth grade? Can this society prosper if it continues to miseducate at least one-third of its graduates?

The questions answer themselves. We Americans cannot succeed, we should not stand by, and society cannot prosper if things go on as they are. Nor will our young people succeed as they mature into adulthood. If citizens, parents, and community leaders do not take action, today's children are going to find tough sledding in their future.

In 1989 the Business Roundtable, of which I was a member, began work on a nationwide campaign to support high and demanding standards for all students. The Roundtable thought the business community should push for raising the education bar. It wanted to improve standards. It wanted graduates who were better fitted for adult life and a society that worked because its citizens were committed to it. Nobody wanted those things more than I did. And I still want them.

That Roundtable agenda persists to this day in statewide efforts to advance reform and in a public awareness campaign known as "Keep the Promise." The television ads in that public awareness campaign relate school standards to everyday adult success. The ads are good-humored and good-natured; audiences invariably smile and laugh when they first see them. One of these ads shows a small Anglo boy struggling to keep the engine from falling off his model airplane; another shows a little African American girl with a stethoscope trying to figure out how to stuff the heart back into the plastic doll on her "operating table." The voice over provides the message to the viewer: Let's hope the engineers designing your airplanes and the surgeons you rely on know what they are doing.

My favorite shows a young boy on the straightaway of a running track preparing to tackle a flight of tiny hurdles. Maybe seven or eight years old, he dances and skips gracefully across the little hurdles, literally doing a pirouette over one, arms akimbo. He is having such a great time that he is fun to watch. But then he encounters a regulation-size high hurdle up to his chin. In front of this imposing obstacle, the boy comes to a perplexed halt. The bar has been raised too high and he cannot clear it. The message is self-evident: Students who have not been challenged in school will come up short when they come across the "real deal," the challenges of daily life in the adult world.

All of this means that it is time to answer the question posed in the 1930s by a great educator, Robert Maynard Hutchins, president of the University of Chicago. "Perhaps the greatest idea America has given to the world," said Hutchins, "is the idea of education for all. The world is entitled to know whether this idea means that everybody can be educated, or that everybody must go to school." I believe that everybody can be educated. Children cannot all learn the same thing, but they can all learn to high and demanding standards. By everybody, I mean the range of typical students found everywhere—every young person in America who is not so disabled by severe handicapping conditions that his or her capacity to learn is flawed.

Everybody can learn. That's the talk we talk, but it is not the walk we walk. Our education system simply requires everyone to go to school. And because most of today's reforms accept that system and the outlook underlying it as a given, they represent little more than well-intentioned efforts to fine-tune failure. The time has come to start walking the talk. Education is fundamental to jobs and to American democracy. We cannot continue to operate a system that turns some children into winners and consigns the rest to the scrap heap. That is simply not acceptable in our economy. And it is not acceptable in this democracy.

We should act in support of our beliefs. The first act is to straighten out the system so that it can do what it is supposed to do. To my amazement, people in the United States do not even agree on what a high school graduate (or a fourth or eighth grader) should know and be able to do.

The next task is to redefine the "public school." I think it should be any nonprofit entity willing to be accountable for educating children. They are acting in the public interest. With that definition in place, education innovation should be hardwired into the system, and as much choice injected as the system can stand.

Finally, we Americans need to face up to how most of us have contributed to the situation. We are in denial about our own role. Like an alcoholic or gambling addict blaming his family for his behavior, many of us like to pretend we would not behave this way if only somebody else did not behave that way. So some citizens turn thumbs down on bond issues to fund schools because they do not like the behavior of today's children, and others fight standards in the name of some misguided commitment to equity or the need to maintain sports eligibility. As citizens—parents, nonparents, business leaders, university officials, and public servants—we do not always support learning either. It is time we changed our ways.

Hard work and difficult decisions lie ahead. Public education needs to be redesigned to save it for the public. It needs to be reshaped to save it from itself. But think of the benefits: a legacy of learning for our children.

Schools:
Good and Getting Better?
Or Bad and Getting Worse?

RONALD REAGAN was not at his best. It was October 1981, and the president, accompanied by James Baker, one of his triumvirate of top aides, was meeting with the members of the National Commission on Excellence in Education in the White House Cabinet Room. As James Harvey, staff director of the commission, shook hands with the president, he was shocked at Reagan's appearance. Despite his makeup, the president was pale; he looked stiff. The famous smile was in place, but he moved with the frail and halting steps of an old man. Harvey remembers being appalled at how weak the president looked. He wondered why the public had not been alerted to his condition and prepared for the worst.

Eighteen months later, when Reagan accepted the commission's report, *A Nation at Risk,* the improvement in his physical appearance was hard to credit. The president literally hopped up onto the low stage from which he was to speak and delivered his prepared text with vigor and confidence.

Only then did Harvey realize what he had been looking at a year and a half before. When Reagan had first met with the excellence commission, he was still recovering from an attempt on his life. In a few violent seconds of gunfire in late March 1981, Reagan had been seriously wounded in the chest; his press secretary, James Brady, struck by a bullet in the brain, had been partially paralyzed. Recovering from his wound had obviously been an ordeal for the president. It had taken much more out of him, Harvey thought, than the public ever knew. On that October day in 1981, six months after the assassination attempt, Reagan was still recovering from it.

Even so, the "Great Communicator" rose to the occasion. Sitting at the Cabinet table, he at first delivered some unexceptional remarks with the help of index cards. "Certainly," he said, "there are few areas of American life as important to our society, to our people, and to our families as our schools and colleges." Commission chairman David Gardner, president of the University of Utah, was expected to respond. Gardner nervously drew an envelope with some handwritten notes from his jacket and humorously laid claim to the right to employ them since the president had already done the same thing. Reagan nodded assent, smiling good-naturedly.

When Gardner finished, Reagan began answering questions from the group, his responses at first aimless and unfocused. Then, without any notable stimulation and even less warning, he suddenly found his voice. What worried him, he said, was that Americans did not expect as much from their students as many other countries expected from theirs.

"You know," said Reagan, with the characteristic deprecating duck of his head, "I was governor of California for eight years. Every year, I met with the best students in the state." In his early years as governor, he recalled, most of these students were native born and Anglo. But as his second term started, he began to notice that more and more of the best students in California were immigrants— mostly Asian and Latin, with a few Europeans tossed in. By the end of the second term, he said, it was hard to find a native Californian. "I was really curious about these foreign students," recalled the president. "And I began asking them how they compared school in their native lands with school here in the United States. And every year, the answer was always the same; it never varied. It didn't matter where they came from—all these foreign students, they just laughed."

The president's story stuck in Harvey's mind. Harvey knew that laughter arose from a mixture of embarrassment and politeness. The students would rather not have been asked the question. Harvey himself had had the same experience as a teenager coming to the United States in the late 1950s from schools in Ireland and England. "I found it easy to disagree with President Reagan on a lot of things," he says, "but he was correct about that. When I was asked as a boy how American schools compared to schools in Ireland and England, I just laughed. Anyone who needed to ask the question would never understand the answer. The comparison was just ridiculous."

A Rising Tide of Mediocrity

Reagan's insight—that expectations for American students and schools are not high enough—became one of the driving forces in the school reform movement of the 1980s as well as one of the major themes of the excellence commission. *A Nation at Risk,* the report the commission delivered to the president on April 24, 1983, was a powerful indictment of the state of American learning.[1] It acknowledged that Americans could justifiably take pride in what their schools had accomplished over the years. It affirmed the importance of educational opportunity and equity. And it made a subtle and important distinction when it noted that although Americans overall are better educated today than were their peers of a generation ago, today's high school graduates are not.

The heart of its message, however, was a firebell in the night. "Our nation is at risk," the commission report began. "The educational foundations of our society are presently being eroded by a rising tide of mediocrity that threatens our very future as a Nation and a people." The commission warned: "If an unfriendly foreign power had attempted to impose on America the mediocre educational performance that exists today, we might well have viewed it as an act of war. . . . We have, in effect, been committing an act of unthinking, unilateral educational disarmament."[2]

In support of this remarkable argument, unprecedented in the history of American schools, the excellence commission pulled together some convincing and troubling evidence:[3]

—International comparisons of student achievement revealed that on nineteen academic tests, American students were never first or second and, in comparison with other industrialized nations, were last seven times.

— Some 23 million American adults were functionally illiterate by the simplest tests of everyday reading, writing, and comprehension.

— About 13 percent of all seventeen-year-olds in the United States could be considered functionally illiterate. Functional illiteracy among minority youth might run as high as 40 percent.

— Average achievement of high school students on most standardized tests had declined over twenty-five years.

— The College Board's Scholastic Aptitude Tests (SATs) demonstrated a virtually unbroken decline from 1963 to 1980. College Board achievement tests also revealed consistent declines in such subjects as physics and English. Moreover, the number and proportion of students demonstrating superior achievement on the SATs had gone down dramatically.

— Science achievement of U.S. seventeen-year-olds, as measured by the National Assessment of Educational Progress (NAEP), had declined steadily since 1969.

Gardner and his colleagues on the commission laid the blame for this state of affairs on a combination of too little time for learning, trivial content that "dumbed" down the curriculum, and minimal expectations for student performance. They theorized that parents, in the interest of minimizing pressure on their children, had often exerted pressure to keep expectations down. And the commission insisted that their conclusions covered the performance of students at both public and private schools.

The commission's report, and the disturbing data on which its argument rested, became the foundation of a nationwide education reform movement that began the following day and continues to this very moment. That reform movement spawned the national education goals developed in 1989 by President Bush and the nation's governors under the leadership of Bill Clinton, then governor of Arkansas. It was the foundation of the America 2000 program developed by Secretary of Education Lamar Alexander and myself on behalf of the Bush administration. And it was the core of the Goals 2000 legislation developed by Secretary of Education Riley and his colleagues in the Clinton administration. In fact, the entire standards-based reform effort of the last decade—the standards championed by the Business Roundtable, the Bush and Clinton administrations, and a great number of scholars and analysts in and out of government and on and off campus—can be traced directly back to *A Nation at Risk*. Practically everything that followed was related in some way to the alarm it sounded.

Some revisionist history has, of course, been written. Represented mostly by stalwarts from the education establishment and schools of education, the revisionists maintain the excellence commission got it wrong. The picture, they say, is not nearly as bleak as the reformers paint it.[4] In fact, many of them imply, if indeed they do not say it outright, these criticisms are not only wrong and misplaced, but part of a malevolent assault on public education.

Which is it? Was the excellence commission correct? Or are its critics right and the excellence commission wrong? As Stanford University faculty members David Tyack and Larry Cuban state the question: Are our schools good and getting better, or are they bad and getting worse?[5]

The National Picture

It is always possible, of course, that revisionists, writing in the 1990s, are describing an educational reality markedly different from the one that confronted the excellence commission a decade earlier. Perhaps by now American schools are, in fact, good and getting better.

On this point the evidence is mixed. The commission caustically criticized the squishy secondary school curriculum followed by many students. Instead of dumbing down the curriculum, the commission said, educators should see to it that every high school graduate is required to complete a challenging academic course of studies involving four years of English, three of science, three of history and social studies, three of mathematics, and half a year of computer science.

Only 13 percent of high school graduates had followed such a course in 1982, according to the National Center for Education Statistics (NCES); ten years later, the percentage had increased dramatically, to 47 percent.[6] "The increase in the number of students taking what the commission defined as the 'new basics' was one of the most significant results of our work," says Milton Goldberg, who served as executive director of the excellence commission.[7] Moreover, according to the same NCES review, other indicators of student performance were also encouraging. The number of students taking advanced placement examinations had increased dramatically; fewer students were taking remedial mathematics (indicating that lower performing students were not suffering from the increased demands); and the dropout rate had declined 5 percent.

More rigorous assessments of what students are learning are not as encouraging. Since 1969 the U.S. Department of Education (and its predecessors) has been conducting a major nationwide review of student learning known as the National Assessment of Educational Progress. Always highly regarded as a rigorous, state-of-the-art assessment of student performance, the NAEP is a nationally representative "snapshot" of academic achievement. Not surprisingly, then, it is known as the "nation's report card."

On a regular and recurring basis, NAEP assesses what nine-, thirteen-, and seventeen-year-old students know in important curricular areas such as reading, writing, mathematics, and science. One of its most useful features is that it permits Americans to monitor trends in academic achievement over extended periods of time. To be precise, it permits comparisons of student performance in science since 1970, in mathematics since 1973, in reading since 1971, and in writing since 1984.

What do these comparisons show about changes in student performance? The results are a mixed bag. Sometimes the scores go up, sometimes they go down. Promising improvements in one assessment cycle are not confirmed by the next one. In particular, the NAEP shows that carrying over improvement in the earlier grades into the secondary years is especially difficult. Here, in summary, are the findings from a recent comprehensive review of NAEP results over the years:[8]

—*Science.* Performance of students in all three age groups declined in the 1970s and recouped slightly afterward.

—*Mathematics.* Mathematics results show a modest improvement for nine- and thirteen-year-olds over the years; unfortunately, the performance of seventeen-year-olds declined from 1973 to 1982, and the average score in 1994 was not significantly different from the 1973 results.

—*Reading.* Overall reading scores for all three ages are practically unchanged since 1971.

— *Writing.* Overall performance of nine- and thirteen-year-olds was practically unchanged between 1984 and 1994, but for seventeen-year-olds, average performance actually declined.

All in all, the NAEP results are hardly encouraging evidence for the revisionists to lean on. Science results look spotty, with the most recent end products (seventeen-year-olds) not doing as well as their peers of a generation ago. The story is similar in math, although some improvement may have occurred since 1990. Little real change has occurred in both reading and writing. What begins to emerge is a pattern of stability, sometimes even modest improvement, for elementary and middle school students in all areas, accompanied by stagnation and sometimes decline for senior high school students. Looked at overall and evaluated without excuses, the NAEP assessments reveal a dreadful possibility: The longer today's American students remain in the school system, the poorer their performance in comparison with their predecessors.

An International Perspective

Perhaps the NAEP results are irrelevant. Valuable as they are, they assess the performance of American students only. How do these students compare with students elsewhere? How do they compare with the successors to the students who could only laugh politely when then-governor Reagan asked them to compare school in the United States with school in their native country?

Internationally, the domestic pattern is strikingly confirmed. Compared with students elsewhere, the performance of American elementary school students is impressive; American middle school students are in the middle of the pack; and American senior high school students are hanging on by their fingernails, just barely.

Two major international assessments lead to these conclusions. The first, released in 1996 by the International Education Assessment, assessed the reading literacy of fourth graders in twenty-seven nations and ninth graders in thirty-one.[9] The second, which is still being released, is the Third International Mathematics and Science Study (TIMSS), the major international education survey of the 1990s. TIMSS assessed nine- and thirteen-year-olds all over the world together with students in the last year of secondary school, no matter what their age was. In the United States the TIMSS assessment involved five different grades (in the United States, grades three and four, seven and eight, and twelve), two distinct curricular areas (mathematics and science), and more than 500,000 students around the world. The American series of reports on this study, entitled *Pursuing Excellence*, is issued by the U.S. Department of Education, which is reporting on one student population at a time. Reports on fourth, eighth, and twelfth graders have been issued, but reports on grades three and seven had not been produced by mid-1999.[10]

In the United States TIMSS involved 585 schools (545 public and 40 private) and 33,339 nine- and thirteen-year-old students and twelfth graders. The designers of the study went to great trouble to make sure that the criticisms of previous international comparisons (including complaints that *all* American students were compared with only the best students in other nations) could not be leveled against TIMSS.

All told, forty-six countries participated in TIMSS, which assessed student performance in more than thirty different languages. Each nation was required to participate in the assessment of thirteen-year-olds; participation in the assessments of younger and older students was encouraged, but discretionary. Because of various technical problems and the voluntary nature of some of the assessments, *Pursuing Excellence* reports on forty-one nations for eighth grade, but only twenty-six for fourth grade, and twenty for twelfth grade.

What the figures reveal in each of the three areas assessed —reading, mathematics, and science—is unambiguous. They are a wake-up call to America. Even with all the appropriate statistical safeguards in place, the data show that the longer American students are in school, the poorer their performance in comparison with their peers abroad.

Based simply on the rank order in which each nation's students wound up, here are what these international surveys reveal. In reading the average score of American students placed them second out of twenty-seven nations at fourth grade, but by ninth grade Americans were in a tie for eighth place. In general science Americans were third out of twenty-six nations at fourth grade, seventeenth of forty-one at eighth grade, and tied for eighteenth out of twenty nations at twelfth grade. In general mathematics the pattern is virtually identical: in fourth grade, Americans ranked twelfth out of twenty-six nations; by eighth grade they had slipped to twenty-eight out of forty-one; and by twelfth grade were tied for eighteenth out of twenty.

Even the most advanced American students do not measure up in international comparisons. They are not world class. The top high school seniors—that small proportion who take physics and advanced mathematics courses such as calculus and analytical geometry— performed much more poorly on the TIMSS tests than similar students elsewhere. Out of twenty nations, none scored significantly lower than the United States in advanced mathematics, and only one (Austria) did so in physics. "Even the very small percentage of students taking Advanced Placement courses are not among the world's best," said William H. Schmidt, the Michigan State University professor who served as national research coordinator for the study in the United States.[11]

Simple rank orders, of course, can be deceptive. On a scale of 0 to 1,000, is there really much of a difference between a reading test score of 534 and one of 535? Like opinion pollsters who estimate the standard error in their polls, American statisticians have published reports documenting statistically significant differences in international achievement. (Using this approach, for example, one can say that only one nation, Korea, indisputably outranks Americans in fourth-grade science. One could also conclude that American ninth graders are tied for second in reading out of thirty-one countries or that their performance is statistically indistinguishable from students in sixteen other nations.) Therefore, the series of American reports called *Pursuing Excellence* likes to report nations' average results as either significantly higher than the United States, not significantly different from the United States, or significantly lower than the United States. Even this more sympathetic definition does not change the picture greatly.

Suppose, without all the statistical whereases and wherefores, the question is framed as follows. According to simple rank orders, where do American students stand on each of these assessments relative to their peers in the other participating nations? At each grade level, are American students ahead of students in 90 percent of the other nations? Fifty percent? Twenty-five percent? Or is the situation worse that that?

FIGURE 2-1

Ranking of Performance of American Students Relative to Their International Peers, by Subject and Grade Level[a]

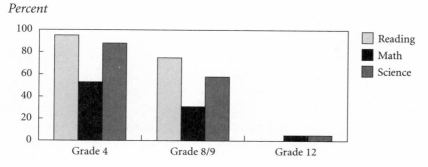

Percent

Sources: National Center for Education Statistics, *Pursuing Excellence* (U.S. Department of Education, 1996, 1997, and 1998); NCES, *Reading Literacy in the United States* (U.S. Department of Education, 1996).

a. The reading literacy assessment involved 27 nations at grade 4; 31 at grade 9; and did not assess twelfth grade reading literacy. Both the science and mathematics assessments involved 26 nations at grade 4, 41 at grade 8, and 20 at grade 12. The assessment of advanced science and mathematics involved only the last year of secondary school.

Based on the discussion so far, it is easy to anticipate that the results for the twelfth grade will not be a pretty picture from the American point of view. In fact, as shown in figure 2-1, they can only be judged intolerable. In everyday terms, the performance of American students compared to the rest of the world goes from near king of the mountain in fourth grade to scraping the bottom of the barrel by twelfth grade. Specifically, in fourth grade the performance of American students exceeds that of about 90 percent of the students in participating countries in two key subjects, reading and science. By the end of secondary school, the picture is reversed: students in 95 percent of participating countries outperform those in the United States in the two subjects assessed, science and mathematics. This is a profoundly disturbing picture.

There is some good news in these international comparisons, particularly in the performance of fourth graders in reading and science. Even in mathematics, the weakest area, American fourth graders are above average. And American eighth graders are also considered to be above average in science, doing much better than many had feared.

But the good news is outweighed by the bad. Very troubling patterns are too clear to miss. Among them:

—The international standing of American students slips in reading, science, and mathematics as they move from fourth to eighth grade, and it slips even further (at least based on the evidence for math and science) as they progress to twelfth grade.

—Even the best students follow this pattern in mathematics. If an international talent search were to select the top 10 percent of all math students in the world, everything else being equal, one would expect to find 10 percent of American students among them. About 9 percent of U.S. fourth graders rank in the world's top 10 percent in math, but by eighth grade only 5 percent do. By twelfth grade, the performance of the best students (the top 14 percent of all seniors) places them in a tie for last place.

—The top 10 percent of American eighth-grade math students perform at about the level of the average student in Singapore. Fully one-fourth of Japanese students score as well as our best.[12]

—The performance of the best American eighth-grade science students is stronger but not good enough. Sixteen percent of fourth graders and 13 percent of eighth graders rank at the top in science. By comparison, 31 percent of Singapore students and 18 percent of those from Japan can be found at the top.

—Mathematics experts consider much of what American eighth graders study in mathematics to be seventh-grade material, while many thirteen-year-olds abroad are already into ninth-grade substance.

—Only one country, the United States, falls from above the international average in mathematics at grade four to below it at grade eight.

I have been in meetings where educators, presented with data such as these, have responded, in effect, "All of that is well and good, but, you see, we educate everyone. These findings don't really mean what you think they mean. Our commitment to equal opportunity requires us to support a system that expects every student to graduate from high school. These other nations support only a small proportion of their students through graduation." That argument has always been a showstopper. When presented with it, I have always found myself acknowledging its validity, despite my misgivings about the performance of our graduates.

Now I find out that the argument is dead wrong. The preeminence of the United States in high school graduation rates is simply a myth. It is an attractive myth, and one that Americans all would like to believe, but it is still a fantasy. Late in 1998 the Paris-based Organization for Economic Cooperation and Development (OECD) issued a report comparing graduation rates in leading industrialized nations. The United States, once thought to be a world leader in high school completion, now trails twenty-two other leading industrial countries in this important area.[13]

It is not the case, apparently, that we are doing worse than we used to, according to the report and its authors. It is that so many other countries are doing so much better. So we find that the United States, with a graduation rate of about 72 percent, is grouped with several other nations in the 70–80 percent range, including Canada, Ireland, Italy, and Spain. As measured by per capita income, several of these countries can draw on only half the wealth of the United States. Meanwhile, nations such as Belgium, Finland, Japan, New Zealand, Norway, Poland, Portugal, and South Korea report high school graduation rates in excess of 90 percent. Little wonder the OECD report concluded that the United States "has lost its supremacy as the premier educator." It is difficult to imagine a sadder conclusion than that.

The important thing to bear in mind in all of these international comparisons is this. Although some progress has undeniably been made, nearly two decades after the excellence commission issued its grim warning about the effects of poor curriculum content and low expectations on student performance, the latest domestic and international findings, far from contradicting the commission, ratify it in practically every important detail.

Facing Up to Reality

Let's be honest. In any complicated area of national life, it is always possible to discount one piece of data or another. But so much evidence of shoddy results in American secondary schools has to be explained away that in the end the explanations lack the power to persuade. Any analyst can convincingly explain why it is a mistake to focus on adult literacy rates as evidence of educational failure—or on the low achievement of inner-city minority students, declines in SAT results, discouraging trends in science assessment results, the poor showing of American students on international achievement tests, or the fact that the United States now trails twenty-two nations in high school graduation rates. But nobody can plausibly explain how all of these things together are irrelevant. Although the individual bits and pieces of the evidence are troubling enough, it is the totality of the evidence that is so devastating.

Facts are stubborn things. The combination of facts about the performance of American students is so overwhelming that a disinterested observer is forced to conclude that something has gone terribly wrong in American schools. Whatever it is, the education system clearly is not working.

In the end, the answer to the question whether American schools are good and getting better or bad and getting worse is in three parts. Elementary schools appear to be pretty solid, but undoubtedly they can be better. Middle schools are holding their own, but just barely. And secondary schools are probably much worse than most of us feared them to be. The national challenge is to make all of these schools better.

Even the good news contained in these averages needs to be tempered. Nobody can pretend that urban elementary schools in the United States are pretty solid. The reverse is true. A book-length report from the highly respected *Education Week* newspaper summarized reading, mathematics, and science scores for students in central city schools and elsewhere in the United States early in 1998. In NAEP's 1994 test of fourth-grade reading, 57 percent of inner-city school children were unable to score at even a basic level and that proportion rose to 77 percent in schools where half or more of the children are poor. In eighth-grade mathematics and science, the story is similar. In math in 1996, 58 percent were unable to score at a basic level, and in high-poverty schools, the proportion reached 67 percent. In science the comparable figures are 62 percent and 69 percent, respectively.

So we should stop kidding ourselves. Even though the fourth-grade averages are encouraging, they conceal almost as much as they reveal.

How have things come to this state? How has it happened that America's legendary schools, renowned throughout the world for pioneering the revolutionary idea of democratic access for all to an education of high quality, are now drowning in a rising tide of mediocrity?

Telltale hints framing an answer to that question are scattered far and wide over the education landscape. Ultimately, most of the hints come back to us, the American people. Broadly united on education in the abstract, we Americans are deeply divided when the abstractions become real students. The schools we have are the schools we want. It is time we created the schools our kids deserve.

CHAPTER THREE

How Did We Get This Way?
Decent Impulses Gone Astray

I HAVE ALWAYS BELIEVED that if the schools will educate, businesses will train. By that I basically mean that it is not an employer's job to teach English grammar, but it is an employer's job to train its employees how to write a business letter. Schools are supposed to teach basic math; businesses should count on them to do that, with the understanding that ongoing employee training can take up specific bookkeeping systems.

Some years ago Jim Harvey raised the old issue of vocational versus academic education in an interesting new way for me. Jim had helped Arnie Packer, director of the Secretary of Labor's Commission on Achieving Necessary Skills, develop the so-called SCANS commission reports.[1] Harvey told me that one night he had expressed his concern to Arnie about the possibility that SCANS might make education too vocational. People might think SCANS was designed to turn schools into career academies, he suggested. Subject matter was being bent out of shape. Pointing with pride to his daughter's success as an off-Broadway playwright, Harvey observed that "Janet had a liberal education as an English major and not the SCANS curriculum or its competencies. Look at how well she's doing."

Packer's response, Harvey said, was that Janet was a starving artist. "When it's time for her to earn a living, she'll have to develop some skills." Packer insisted that SCANS was not about doing away with traditional curriculum; it was about enriching it with practical projects emphasizing skills such as teamwork and data analysis. Time for these projects, Packer said, could be found by redoing the curriculum to match new realities. One of his points was that the widespread availability of calculators made teaching arithmetic a waste of time. Multiplication tables? Who needs them? Cosines? Developed to help nineteenth-century artillery officers calculate elevation angles for their cannons. Mental discipline? Transferable skills? Nonsense. "Nothing more than mental calisthenics, gymnastics that don't transfer into improved performance," Packer maintained.

That discussion reproduced in miniature, in about ten minutes, much of the centuries-long debate about the purposes of American education. Is it about learning or life? Is there something valuable on a human scale in knowledge for its own sake? Or do starving artists need to learn something practical if they are to earn a living? What exactly is it that American society is trying to accomplish through public schools in the United States? If business is truly to train, what should it expect from American schools by way of education?

Progressive and Decent Impulses

Go to an education meeting anywhere in the United States today, drop the phrase "the American common school," and listen as a reverent hush descends on the room. Some eyes will probably mist over. So powerful is this image of schools that advanced democracy by taking in every child, American-born and immigrant alike, treating them all the same, and turning every child out prepared to take his or her place in the world that educators continue to appeal to it, even though most of them know it never really existed. The common school has a mystical appeal, a totemic quality; it is an education icon.

But the common school is not to be scorned. In a very special way, it lived as a representation of some of the most decent and progressive impulses of the American people. It existed as an ideal in the mind's eye of visionaries who saw in it a mechanism for realizing all the possibilities America promised the world. Just because it never truly existed does not mean it wasn't real. And just because these visionaries could not bring it fully into being does not mean their conception did not have powerful effects.

For all its difficulties, American education can demonstrate a record of expansion, of providing opportunity for more and more education to more and more people. Public schools helped make much of the progress of twentieth-century America possible. People on Main Street understand that intuitively, which is one reason they recoil from some of the harsher rhetoric emanating from today's reform camps.

Everyone today takes the American public school for granted, but in its current incarnation—secular and accessible to all—it is a very recent creation, only about forty years old.[2] And today's school began with a vision of a common school. This is what the histories and official statistics tell us:

—From the birth of the Republic, education has been one of the great engines of American democracy. In colonial America, Latin and Greek "grammar schools" prepared a small elite for college, and voluntary "academies" provided social mobility for a few others.[3]

—Massachusetts' 1647 "Old Deluder Satan Law," which distinguished between elementary reading-and-writing schools (sometimes called petty schools) and more advanced grammar schools, ordered communities to support petty schools because Satan's chief project was "to keep men from the knowledge of the Scriptures."[4]

—In the 1760s Benjamin Franklin advocated English-language schools to unify communities and to nip in the bud the expansion of the German culture of many new immigrants.[5]

—The Northwest Ordnance of 1787 set aside land for schools in what is today the Upper Midwest.

—Beginning in the 1840s, after several Catholic churches were burned on the East Coast during the Know-Nothing riots, Irish-Americans, their religious beliefs threatened, abandoned public schools and set up their own parochial school system. Even before the church burnings, Catholics viewed the "public schools" with their Protestant bible, prayers, and hymns to be "Protestant schools," not just passively against their religion, but actively hostile to it.[6]

—The "common school" advocated by Horace Mann and his allies in the mid-nineteenth century was designed to encourage equal education for all in a schoolhouse shared in common and to promote state supervision and regulation of schools.[7]

—Well into the twentieth century, public education for most people meant elementary education. Fully one-quarter of adults over age twenty-five had completed just five years or less of school in 1910. As late as 1960 fewer than half of all American adults had completed four years of high school.[8]

This Cook's tour of the education history of the United States reveals that most of the dilemmas that schools face today have been present from the outset. Throughout American history, dueling orthodoxies have contended over whether schools should educate an elite or everyone; focus on content or stress process; insist on the use of English or be ecumenical about language; concentrate on knowledge for its own sake or worry about employability; provide a base of common knowledge for all or offer something for everyone; or promote religious belief or celebrate the secular state. In the debate on the role of American education, there is nothing new under the sun.

This history reveals something else as well. Today's public school system is an outgrowth of a system established to manage elementary schools. Although considerable thought was given to the relationship between elementary and secondary education, secondary schools were simply grafted onto the elementary administrative apparatus without a great deal of planning and without anyone really questioning whether that was a sensible thing to do.

Against that backdrop, it is easy to understand how several factors converged to produce today's schools. It is all too tempting to lay the blame for the current state of affairs at the feet of a handful of actors in the education drama—to blame self-centered superintendents, meddling boards, disinterested parents, or recalcitrant unions. In fact, I cannot resist the temptation myself and will examine their roles in greater detail in the following chapters. Here, I want to take in the bigger picture and look at the great movements that shaped the schools. How did they get that way?

It seems to me that three factors are key: unwillingness to define precisely what society wanted from the schools; the triumph of a cult of efficiency and professionalism that succeeded in creating large and impersonal schools, particularly at the secondary level; and the careless decision to open and administer secondary schools with an apparatus built to create and manage elementary schools.

Intellectual Development or Preparation for Life?

From colonial times, a debate has persisted in American schools, becoming most publicly evident in the last 100 years. Should public schools develop the intellect? Or is their purpose to prepare students for life? Ideally, they do both. But professional educators have tended to offer different answers for different students: different strokes for different folks.

Initially a subject of discussion primarily among educators, this debate began to attract considerable public attention in the 1890s. In 1892 the "Committee of Ten," a group of college presidents supported by the National Education Association, issued a statement calling for a liberal, academic course of secondary school studies for all; this recommendation was resoundingly rejected by a commission of professional educators, also sponsored by the National Education Association.[9] The second group called instead for meeting the needs of students and preparing them for the real world they would enter. The second statement was a triumph of public relations. It is very hard to find anyone, including myself, who is opposed to "preparing students for the real world."

Today, a century later, the dispute has again burst into the open, in almost identical terms. The excellence commission's 1983 report (calling for a liberal, academic course of secondary school studies for all) was followed within a few years by the SCANS Commission, which argued for preparing students for the real world by improved preparation for work.

My friend Diane Ravitch has thought a lot about this issue. Ravitch is a distinguished academic who left Columbia University to serve in the Bush administration as assistant secretary for education research and improvement and is now affiliated with both New York University and the Brookings Institution. She argues that pedagogical progressivism, devoid of content, has been the philosophic well from which the education profession has drawn for much of this century. Progressive ideas, she says, "inverted [John] Dewey's notion of the-school-as-a-lever-of-social-reform into the-school-as-a-mechanism-to-adjust-the-individual-to-society. . . ."[10] Inverting Dewey or not, these principles became the cornerstone of education thinking, for both elementary and secondary schools, in twentieth-century America.

Progressive educators dismissed as nonsense the theory of improving intellectual functioning by studying specific subjects, Ravitch says. Instead progressives argued that what is learned is not nearly as important as the process of learning how to learn. Their position was that a student should not study content to learn how to think, but should learn how to think and then select the content he or she wants to learn.

What developed, according to Ravitch, was a pronounced shift away from schooling as intellectual development and the mastery of subject matter. The social and emotional development of students became a major preoccupation of the curriculum, which also supported functional activities related to vocation, health, and family life. Instead of balancing the intellectual, social, and emotional needs of students in school, educators set out consciously to denigrate the idea of "knowledge for its own sake." In place of common demanding standards, educators set out to diversify curriculum because, in the words of one typical professor of education, diversification meets "the needs of children of mediocre or inferior ability who lack interest in abstract and academic materials."[11]

By the 1950s progressivism as a philosophy of education was dead, but its memory lingered on. For example, in 1997 a New England professor of education told researchers from the Public Agenda Foundation, "You can be a lifelong learner and learn the things you don't know in terms of the content. . . ." In other words, once you have the process down, you can learn anything that interests you. This philosophy is so convenient it is almost too good to be true. And what it produced was the worst of all worlds: a generation of teachers and administrators raised on intellectual pabulum, on an incoherent theory that explicitly rejected rigorous intellectual development in favor of feel-good projects designed to promote social and emotional development.

The Cult of Efficiency and Professionalism

Paul Hill, a University of Washington political scientist who, while at the RAND Corporation, helped with the first years of New American

Schools, often describes a profoundly troubling visit he made to a New York City high school in the late 1980s.[12] He was analyzing why some public high schools seemed to work well, while others did not, and comparing the two types with each other and also with parochial high schools in the city.[13] He was beginning to be convinced that student anonymity and alienation in large, bureaucratic, and impersonal schools and school systems was one of the issues involved.

Speaking with the vice principal of a large public school early one afternoon, Hill noticed several dozen young men and women outside on the street, smoking, chatting, and carrying on quite loudly the way teenagers do. The noise came in through the open window of the school office. Periodically, cars filled with teenagers, their stereos blaring, arrived and left, adding to the confusion. Some of the drivers held short, impromptu drag races. Distracted, Hill said, more to himself than anyone else: "Who are those kids?" To his surprise the vice principal immediately answered: "Those are our students. They've 'ditched' for the day."[14] Startled, Hill asked why his host didn't go out into the street and herd them into class. Back came the answer: "We're better off with them out there than in here. In here, they only cause trouble."

The image of the ideal American school is of an institution that is small and personal. That is one reason the education orthodoxy of local control of schools is supported so vigorously. The idea is that local control will ensure that schools are oriented to local needs. Although local control may have served as political cover to fend off federal control, it meant nothing at all when standardization of practice and schooling became a professional imperative. Worshiping at the altar of local control for political reasons resulted in the creation of cookie-cutter schools all over the nation in the name of professionalism. And most of these schools became much too big.

The story begins with the numbers. When I was born in 1930 there were about 119,000 school districts in the United States that administered some 238,000 elementary schools and nearly 24,000 secondary schools.[15] Enrollment in the prewar years of the 1930s was about 25 million.[16] By 1994, the number of school districts had decreased to fewer than 15,000, and it has not stopped dropping since. These districts oversee about 64,000 elementary schools and 24,000 secondary schools, enrolling, all told, nearly 45 million students (table 3-1).

TABLE 3-1
Enrollment Growth Combined with Consolidation
of Districts and Schools, 1930–1995

Year	Districts	Elementary schools	Secondary schools	Students
1930	119,000[a]	238,306	23,930	25,678,000
1995	14,883	63,961	23,793	44,840,000

Source: National Center for Education Statistics, *Digest of Education Statistics* (U.S. Department of Education, 1997).
   a. 1937–38.

In other words, since the 1930s nationwide enrollments have increased by about 75 percent, while the number of school districts has fallen by nearly 90 percent and the number of schools by about 67 percent. Clearly the districts got much bigger—and so did the schools. What is not apparent from table 3-1 is that enrollments in the average secondary school just about tripled during this period. In 1930 enrollment in grades nine through twelve was just under 4.4 million; by 1995 it had ballooned to slightly more than 12.2 million.[17] In the face of this enrollment boom, the number of secondary schools actually declined slightly.

Much of this downward shift in the number of schools and school districts occurred in the name of "consolidation" and efficiency. The idea was that small districts, particularly in rural areas, could not provide as comprehensive an array of education services to their students as could larger districts. Why not consolidate and obtain the economies of scale made possible by larger size? My friend Denis Doyle was one of the first people to point out one of the flaws in that argument. In the early 1970s he began arguing that as a result of consolidation, the school as a focus of community hopes, as a meeting center, and as a place to rally around local athletic teams had simply disappeared in many rural areas.[18]

Much of this consolidation also resulted from what Stanford University researchers David Tyack and Larry Cuban describe as a drive by education leaders to shape education policy through science and managerial efficiency and to "take politics out of schools." They thought, according to Tyack and Cuban, "that schooling should be both more differentiated and more standardized: differentiated in curriculum to fit the backgrounds and future destinies of students; and standardized with respect to buildings and equipment . . . and other professional practices."[19]

To buffer schools from what the professionals considered to be the ignorant meddlers on school boards, many alleged to be corrupt and politically motivated, the mavens of administrative efficiency called for reducing the size of lay boards, professionalizing staff, delegating decisions to professionals, and consolidating and standardizing schools.[20]

Standardization has been particularly effective. No matter where one travels in the United States, most of the schools look alike. They practically smell alike. According to Tyack and Cuban, state legislation, regulations, and decisions of state superintendents set the norms for school standardization. Such norms govern the quality and safety of buildings, the qualifications of teachers, the length of the school term, even acceptable playground space and equipment. The demands for standardization by the mandarins of the professionalization movement require a level of uniformity among schools across the nation, reinforced by private accreditation agencies, that takes the breath away. It is no wonder all schools look and smell alike.

The effects of this cult of efficiency, professionalism, and standardization are easy enough to see:

—Early in this century, the "modal" high school had perhaps 100 students, according to Tyack and Cuban; today it enrolls more than 1,000. (Modal means that half of the schools enroll fewer students and half enroll more.) Think about that: enrollment in the typical high school now is about ten times larger than it was less than a century ago.

—According to the National Center for Education Statistics, nearly 2,500 elementary schools enrolled more than 1,000 students in 1994–95; meanwhile, about 2,200 high schools enrolled more than 1,500 students.[21]

—Between 1930 and 1980, Tyack and Cuban report, the number of one-room schools nose-dived from 130,000 to fewer than 1,000.

—And, they say, bureaucracy increased. At the turn of the century there was one staff member in state departments of education for every 100,000 students; by 1974 there was one for every 2,000. Regulations also blossomed. A California education code of two hundred pages at the turn of the century increased to twenty-six hundred pages by 1985.

All of this in the name of progress. In truth, wonderful organizational charts for school systems have been created that look—on paper—as though they might work or might conceivably have worked at one time. On these charts, teachers report to department chairmen and chairwomen. Department leaders, in turn, report to principals, who are viewed as an extension of the central office. Principals report to the superintendent (or in large systems to an assistant superintendent who reports to the superintendent). And the superintendent reports to the board.

Unhappily, it is very hard to make what looks so neat and orderly on paper actually work in practice. Particularly in large school districts, while all of this reporting is going on, no one is genuinely responsible for what actually happens. At the same time, schools have become so large that, quite literally, no one is able to know all the students.

A lot of people worry about this. Many of them are educators so appealing and straightforward in their style that parents and policymakers immediately recognize that they know what they are talking about. In 1985 three researchers—Arthur Powell, Eleanor Farrar, and David K. Cohen—worried that what they called "shopping mall high schools," with their boutiques of offerings to suit every taste, were making winners out of some young people and losers out of others.[22] In a brilliant and provocative book published a few years later, journalist Gerald Grant worried that educators in contemporary comprehensive high schools had retreated so far behind a facade of legalisms that they had disavowed their responsibilities for intellectual development, ignored character development, and no longer possessed the moral authority to promote a sense of school community.[23]

Deborah Meier is today's embodiment of these anxieties. The founding principal of Central Park East, an alternative secondary school in New York City, and currently principal of one of the new Pilot Schools, the public school charters being launched with the support of the Boston teachers' union, Meier is a font of educational wisdom and common sense. When I was deputy secretary of education, she told me that the real task of schools is to provide each student with at least one adult—an administrator, a teacher, a coach, even a custodian or receptionist—who really knows that student. Meier believes schools have become too big if the principal cannot gather all the faculty members around a table and know that every teacher knows every student in the school—maybe twenty teachers responsible for a school of about 400 students.

Debbie Meier is on the right track. Contrast her attitude with the situation that exists in most schools: The cult of efficiency and professionalism has made schools so large, bureaucratic, and impersonal that educators actually say of their students: "We're better off with them out there than in here. In here, they only cause trouble."

Casual Decisions about Secondary School Administration

Recall the history outlined above: The American common school was an elementary school focused on the basic function of teaching the "three R's" and citizenship. The appealing ideology of the common school developed around elementary classrooms. Until the twentieth century, most Americans left school at the end of their elementary education; the high school was an elite institution, serving only a small minority of American youth. Then, as the twentieth century progressed, schools saw not only the development of the progressive ideology and the cult of efficiency, but also an astonishing increase in the number of students enrolled in and graduating from secondary schools. Yet with little thought or preparation, the administration of secondary schools was turned over to a structure originally developed to administer elementary school programs.

Preschool programs known as kindergartens were created by another group of reformers toward the end of the nineteenth century; these, too, were put under the wing of people with little interest in, or understanding of, the needs of infants and very young children. The result: the public accepts the current system of primary and secondary education as though its existence had been preordained.

Nothing was inevitable about any of this. Given some attention and forethought, state policymakers might conceivably have established an entirely different public delivery system for universal access to secondary schools. Recognizing that the common school philosophy was almost a perfect fit with the needs and imperatives of elementary schools, policymakers might also have anticipated that a quite different set of imperatives needed to be met as compulsory education was extended into the turbulent adolescent years. But that did not happen. In a thoughtless, almost cavalier manner, the administration of secondary schools was put in the hands of an elementary school bureaucracy, one raised on the principles of the common schools, dedicated to notions of standardization and consolidation, and trained at the knees of progressives with their scarcely concealed contempt for content.

And so we have the paradox of standardization combined with differentiation at the secondary school level—intensive efforts to standardize buildings and practice and equally intense efforts to provide an array of different content. In developing secondary schools, champions of the common school behaved as though its philosophy could be respected in form by having students enter the same building, where its tenets could be ignored in practice as students were channeled into different curricular tracks.

Course offerings in these diverse education tracks—college preparatory, commercial, vocational, and general—multiplied rapidly. In 1890, according to Tyack and Cuban, statistics on secondary school course enrollments could be gathered under just nine headings; by 1973 high school principals reported more than 2,100 different names for courses as the shopping mall high school offered something for everyone.[24]

What happened? As progressives addressed the challenge of providing universal access to secondary education—the challenge of providing more and more students with more and more education—they found themselves confronting the great democratic dilemma. That dilemma can be stated as follows: Does democratic education imply common materials, courses, curricula, standards, and education for all? Or does democratic education consist of making sure that everyone benefits educationally, even if not equally, implying that courses, offerings, curricula, materials, and standards should be modified to accommodate students' interests and abilities? Hutchins, of course, said it so much better: Do we mean that everyone can be educated, or do we simply mean that everyone must go to school?

Yet, if the common school had stood for anything at all, it had stood for common content and standards. Unfortunately, the secondary school curricula that emerged as the twentieth century developed revealed that given a choice, the inheritors of the vision of Horace Mann and John Dewey practically always elected modification and differentiation.

In support of this approach, says Ravitch, professional educators frequently appealed to dubious science, tentative research, and "laws of learning" to justify tests that divided students into ability groups and to advocate that discipline-bound subject matter give way to projects, interdisciplinary studies, and activities designed to maintain student interest at high levels.

The professional ideal that emerged could not contemplate high standards for all students. It was simply beyond the imagination of most professionals to believe that a demanding secondary school education of the sort that was good enough for the children of the well-to-do was also good enough for the children of the poor. When push came to shove and they were faced with the proposition that most students can learn practically anything, educators balked. They are still balking.

CHAPTER FOUR

What Specifically Is Wrong?

WHEN HOWARD FULLER TALKS, people usually listen. Lean and intense, with a dazzling smile, Fuller still moves with the easy grace that marked his basketball career at Carroll College in Waukesha, Wisconsin in the 1960s, when athletics were a major route out of poverty for many young African American men. Fuller long ago left basketball behind. But not for a second did he forget the plight of the young black men and women with whom he had grown up.

When Fuller describes his experiences as superintendent of Milwaukee's schools, he speaks calmly and evenly. His is an easy manner. He has somehow mastered the art of getting into people's faces without threatening them. Every gesture communicates that he has no quarrel to pick with the people in the room. He speaks more in sadness than in anger; he smiles to minimize the force of the passion behind his position. Only occasionally does a mild tremor in his voice or a slight quiver in his mustache reveal just how hard he works to keep his rage under control.

What he has to say about urban schools is an invitation to revolution. "We're sending kids to their educational death. When I was superintendent, everyone knew that nothing was going on in some of those schools. Yet year after year we kept sending kids into them. We all knew that nobody had learned anything in these schools for years and that probably nobody ever would. But nothing changed. There was the smell of death and defeat in these schools. Everyone knew it and nobody cared—either inside or outside the system."[1]

Although he served from 1991 to 1995 as Milwaukee superintendent, Fuller is far from a typical educator. In fact he was not a public school educator at all. He worked as a field representative in community and union organizations for years. While obtaining a doctorate at Marquette University, he worked his way up the ranks of the city and state human services bureaucracy in Milwaukee before being asked to run the city's schools. "The legislature had to pass a special law to let me take the job," he chuckles. "I hadn't taken all the education courses required to be a superintendent."

From his current perch directing the Institute for the Transformation of Learning at Marquette, Fuller favors "busting up" the monolithic one-size-fits-all school systems that characterize today's public education and replacing them with "systems of schools." "I knew I was finished in Milwaukee," he says, "the day I told a room full of educators, many of them African American, that I would no longer accept the idea that my major responsibility was to run an employment service for adults. I asked them to join me in accepting the responsibility for seeing to it that our kids learn."

A new school board ousted Fuller, ostensibly because he favored a modest school choice plan backed by a former welfare mother in the state legislature, Polly Williams. But Fuller is convinced that the board, elected with teacher union support, pushed him out simply because he refused to stop talking in public about the disastrous state of urban schools and the need to provide inner-city children and their families with greater choice.

Most Americans are not too surprised when the more conservative elements in a community come out in favor of choice. They take it in stride when groups like the Heritage and Fordham foundations support choice. They do not think it at all odd that statewide Republican parties do what the Michigan Republicans recently did and overwhelmingly endorse tuition tax credits for public elementary and secondary education. Developments that would have appeared unthinkable a decade ago, such as passage of statewide tax credits and voucher programs in places like Arizona, Minnesota, Ohio, and Wisconsin, now merit barely a second glance. Milwaukee and Cleveland are experimenting with vouchers? Of course. What else would one expect?

But the involvement of people like Howard Fuller in the choice movement is genuine news. Something more than conservative politics is at work. Once, the debate about the merits of school choice was largely theoretical; today, the debate is largely over. Support for choice spans a wide ideological range.

In many ways, educators have brought the choice movement on themselves. Insisting that what David Tyack has archly called the "one best system" is the only way to support the public interest in education, educators and educational theorists looked inward at their own interests and not outward. They were happy to stand pat, convinced that little needed to change. This attitude played itself out in innumerable ways, often leading to inertia, if not paralysis. For example, parents and teachers have been teaching children to read since the alphabet was invented. But somehow modern educators ignited a holy war over dueling philosophies of reading in which advocates of phonics (sounding out letters and words) duke it out with supporters of language recognition (an approach emphasizing the recognition of whole words). This is an absurd argument to noneducators, most of whom remember using both approaches at different stages as they themselves learned to read or helped their children learn to read; yet debates like this one are capable of tying up schools and school boards for months at a time.

Even educators' terms have become grist for educational paralysis. In the 1970s some education theorists began to describe their curriculum reform as "outcomes-based education," or OBE for short. That term is typical of the dreadful jargon educators continually use. OBE, like Mark Twain's quip about Wagner's music, was not as bad as it sounds—it means little more than "results." But it was not much good either. It was a good deal of fluff pretending to be standards. It invited criticism, which it swiftly received. OBE quickly became a talisman on the right for everything that is wrong with American schools.[2] It was such a lightening rod, in fact, that when the Business Roundtable used the word "outcomes" in its standards-based reform agenda, it found itself battling well-organized local community groups intent on restoring the "basics" to schools. Roundtable leaders were thunderstruck.[3] That's what they thought they had been doing. The sad thing about the whole story is that the OBE wars gave standards a bad name in some circles.

Whether it is school choice, reading, or terrible education jargon, on issues such as these, schools have remarkably few mechanisms to accommodate people seeking flexibility or variation. Rather than salving their wounds by being responsive, public officials often end up rubbing salt in them by stonewalling.

For when it comes to today's public schools, too often it is an administrative case of one-size-fits-all. Public schools are where Henry Ford was in the 1920s, when he remarked that customers could have their new Model A painted any color they wanted, as long as it was black. Parents are told that their children can have any kind of education the parents want, as long as it is the one the schools are prepared to provide. This reluctance to accommodate differences is one of the central paradoxes of American education. In a society that prizes individual liberty, and in schools that value and respect individual differences, we have created a school governance system oriented around the notion that students have to fit into the limited number of molds that the school bureaucracy is willing to provide.

Nearly two decades of work on school reform have produced little in the way of tangible results. New programs, different curricula, detailed accountability schemes, site-based management, and more money all appear to have had little effect. Why is this so? I think four major factors are at work: the dead weight of the past; process as an excuse for poor performance; sheer inertia; and the dysfunctional family that the American school has become.

The Dead Weight of the Past

The first challenge is the dead weight of American education's past. I think of this dead weight as the "Six Cs"—comfort, complacency, conflict, cowardice, the courts, and a command-and-control mentality.

Let's take comfort. Most people in education—students, parents, teachers, and administrators—are like people everywhere. Change is hard. They really do not want to have to go to all that trouble. Everyone supports change—so long as someone else does the changing.

Ironically, America's past educational success contributes to the comfort levels. Everyone assumes that the sources of past successes—public support and a commitment to public education as we have known it—will continue to be the seeds of future triumphs. So no one wastes a lot of time dwelling on failures or reflecting on mistakes. Everyone prefers to think that if it worked well before, it will work just fine again. Schools have become a lot like businesses in the post-war era. Just as American firms in the 1960s assumed they owned their customers and had nothing to learn from them, American educators in the 1990s behave as though the public will remain loyal, no matter how much the public trust is abused.

The second issue is complacency. Americans like to believe that while something may be true in some communities, it is not true of their own. The common attitude is: Schools in general are in trouble, but "the schools in my community are fine." We're just much too complacent about where our schools and our children stand.

Here, I think some distinctions need to be made. Newspaper columnist William Raspberry told me in 1997 that the challenges facing urban, rural, and suburban schools are different in kind, complexity, and degree.[4] Yet most of us talk about them as if they were all the same. My guess is that Raspberry is right and that Americans must learn to make at least two distinctions. First, I think there needs to be across-the-board improvement in the academic skills of high school graduates. But undoubtedly the schools and students needing the most improvement are in low-income urban and rural areas. Likewise, while education failures can be found at all levels of schooling, the data reviewed in chapter 2 reveal that these failures are undoubtedly the greatest in the middle and secondary school years. Yet, many of us are inclined to tar all levels of schooling with the same brush, a sort of referred pain from our secondary school problems. Reformers' unwillingness to make these distinctions undermines their credibility.

The third "C" is conflict. For the most part, the active participants in the education discussion tend to talk past each other. They take extreme positions, and they yell at each other a lot. The debate is mired in a destructive circle of charges and denials with everyone pointing the finger of blame at the next person in the circle. Reformers condemn all public schools; educators defend them all. Liberals sabotage the Bush administration's effort to implement the national education goals, and conservatives undermine the Clinton administration's attempts to do the same thing. Most reforms have largely ignored the concerns of parents. Administrators have ignored the very real worries of teachers. Until very recently union leaders have dismissed complaints about teacher quality—and some of them still do.

The fourth problem is cowardice. The great coach of the Green Bay Packers football team, Vince Lombardi, used to say "fatigue makes cowards of us all." He was talking about physical weariness, but psychological fatigue grinds people down too. In the face of opposition, most of us become hesitant, timid, afraid to follow our instincts. I am convinced that fear has hamstrung many business and community leaders. But political leaders, too, are unsure of where their followers are going. So they have been satisfied for the most part to tread water as well.

I have to say, too, that fear and anxiety characterize the education establishment. Its members talk a good game of reform, but in the end most of them are willing to support only tiny, timid, baby steps. Nobody ever accused Al Shanker, the late head of the American Federation of Teachers, of being timid. Shanker used to say that schools were never going to be reformed simply by adding a little more of what has already failed and trying to do more of the same—only a little harder and a little better.[5] Shanker was right; many of the fixes advanced for the schools are little more than Band-Aids. We are trying to fine-tune a bad process—the basic structure and organization of the schools themselves—and as long as we do nothing but fine-tune it, we're never really going to change anything at all.

Next, I want to cite the courts. About twenty years ago, Arthur Wise, a RAND Corporation researcher, published an analysis of how government mandates, system regulations, and court decrees of one kind or another tied the schools' hands.[6] But the issue very quickly disappeared. It is not good form to be seen as a critic of the judicial system, which, in fact, has done a lot of good things for American education.

So one almost never reads about this in the reform literature, but efforts to change the status quo in schools frequently run up against the courts and legalisms. Discipline a student without a hearing? See you in court. Hold Johnny back until he learns to read? My lawyer will be in touch. Distinguish between distributing hard drugs on school grounds and offering a friend an aspirin on the school bus? Not a chance—automatic suspension for both crimes. On the advice of lawyers, schools consider themselves to be tightly bound by rules and regulations governing how they treat students.

In Philadelphia the reform plans of the latest superintendent, David Hornbeck, were stymied for months by a local judge with her own ideas about preschool education. In St. Louis the 250 children living in one small complex of 150 units of public housing until 1998 attended forty-three different schools, all in order to satisfy desegregation guidelines. The finances of Cleveland's schools are in such disarray that the schools are in receivership under a court-appointed master. As these examples show, courts are often very powerful arbiters of what schools can and cannot do, particularly in urban areas. Very few people ever acknowledge that.

Finally, across the board in American schools there is a command-and-control mentality. This outlook starts with the proposition that decisions need to be made at the top. It insists that school principals are management extensions of the superintendent and central office, education's foremen really. It holds that teachers cannot really be trusted. It is management by decree, a form of management Taylorism that American corporations long ago abandoned.

The command-and-control outlook means that budgets are determined and controlled in the central office.[7] It means that teacher hiring is a shambles, with teachers centrally hired and new teachers often assigned to schools at the very last minute, sight unseen.[8] Curriculum is set in detail by the district or the state. School boards meet until midnight to decide whether to reroute a school bus or move $5,000 from one account to another in a $500 million budget. Administrators and union leaders measure to the minute how long the school day should be, along with each class period in it, the lunch break, and the precise time teachers are expected to arrive and depart. Bean counters track every dollar to its source. All of this effort dedicated to upholding the letter of the law, whatever its spirit, while student performance is largely ignored or its deficiencies explained away.

There is so little autonomy at the school level that, as a former business executive, I am not sure it makes any sense to ask teachers and principals to accept responsibility for their own performance—they control hardly any of the conditions under which they are expected to produce.

Process as an Excuse for Poor Performance

The second major factor that has stymied school reform is the reverence for process held by bureaucrats, educators, and lawyers. It is because public schools have become bureaucratic enterprises, not community institutions dedicated to raising children, that the Howard Fullers of the world find them so frustrating. Buffeted by decisions made in the political arena and hamstrung by programs and regulations enacted to improve matters, school leaders have, for the most part, retreated into "process" as a defense against charges of education failure.

Educators' excuses for poor school performance, particularly for their failures to educate individual children, are endless. Most are grounded in process, in the claim that they followed the rules and did everything they were supposed to or could conceivably have been expected to do. It is expressed in excuses such as these:

— We know Mary's test results are disappointing, but we followed the curriculum approved by the school board and used the textbooks sanctioned by the state.

— We can't explain why Johnny can't read; he was placed in a compensatory education program.

— Gabriella should be doing better; we provided a bilingual placement.

— We're surprised Hakeem is still acting out; we developed an individual education plan for him.

Explicitly each of these excuses carries the message that the school is legally and bureaucratically impregnable; it did what it was required to do. Implicitly the message to parents is more subtle and incalculably more corrosive: If the prescribed treatment didn't work, it's not our fault. It's probably the student's—and it might be yours.

Sheer Inertia

Next, I want to point to the problem of inertia in big systems. According to David Tyack, education reforms recycle. If you wait around long enough, he told a group of school superintendents in San Francisco in 1996, you see them appear, and disappear, and then appear again. Some features of schooling are just very hard to change, he says.

"Why is what we call the 'grammar of instruction' so persistent in schools?" Tyack asked. "By grammar of instruction, I mean the way schools are organized—the graded school, the fifty-minute periods, the disciplinary breakdowns into English, history, arithmetic, and the like, the emphasis on Carnegie Units, and all the rest of it."[9]

"It's just very hard to change all of that," Tyack continued, "because schools and the larger community are very resistant to change. Most adult Americans have been to school and know what a 'real school' looks like. Parents don't want to hear about ungraded classrooms or interdisciplinary study. For most parents, a real school has a third-grade class in which arithmetic is studied. That's what they had, and it's what they think their kids should have."

Another part of the problem, according to Tyack's Stanford colleague Larry Cuban, is that reformers ignore the actual, practical nature of the classroom and the problems reform proposals create for teachers. Teachers are the gatekeepers of reform, Cuban says. With or without reform, they have a nearly impossible job, encompassing a never-ending sequence of often contradictory demands from students, parents, administrators, local employers, community leaders, and taxpayers.

"In order to do all they have to do, they make decisions about how they will spend their time and what they think is important," Cuban told the superintendents in San Francisco. For a very long time now, technology, for example, has been suggested as the solution to the nation's education problems. First, it was radio, then film strips, then television, followed by computer-assisted instruction, and now the information superhighway. But none of this technology has taken hold in the classroom because teachers are leery of it. "Teachers are inclined to ask very straightforward questions about every new proposal that comes before them. Take technology. Is it simple? Can it be used right now in my classroom? Will it break down? If it does, will I be expected to fix it? Will I look silly if it doesn't work? Above all, will it diminish my authority to maintain order in the classroom by making students independent of me?"

Moreover, according to Tyack and Cuban, schools have developed the capacity to absorb proposed changes and reform the reforms. "People usually ask how reform changes schools," observed Tyack. "Sometimes you need to examine the reverse: how schools change reforms." Some major reforms appear to be adopted, but then they are slowly transformed by the institution that absorbed them. The reformers who created kindergartens and junior high school, said Tyack and Cuban, intended them to be very distinctive kinds of institutions, quite different from the public schools in which they were placed. Instead, they have essentially become additional rungs in the elementary and secondary school ladder, often hardly distinguishable from traditional classrooms.

In the end, they conclude in their book, *Tinkering toward Utopia*, that many innovations appear to shrivel up and die the minute they touch the institutional reality of the school.[10] It is only the very rare reform that persists according to plan. Schools are a kind of "Bermuda Triangle" into which good ideas mysteriously disappear, sometimes never to be heard from again.

The Dysfunctional School Family

The dead weight of tradition, process, and inertia are not the full story. The remaining major challenge is that internally American public schools are like huge dysfunctional families. Within them, hardly anyone trusts anyone else. And, like most dysfunctional families, the remarkable thing is not that schools sometimes fail, but that they ever work at all.

Researchers for Public Agenda Foundation went into four school districts in 1994 to examine the politics of school reform, and they were startled by what they found. (Public Agenda was founded in the early 1980s by public opinion analyst Daniel Yankelovich and former secretary of state Cyrus Vance to help citizens understand important policy issues.) The researchers were prepared to find educators dispirited by outside critics. What confounded them was the complete lack of trust within the school family. According to Public Agenda's John Immerwahr, who is also a philosophy professor at Villanova University, none of the factions responsible for the schools—school boards, parent groups, teachers, unions, principals, or administrators—trusted each other. Organized around narrow interests, competing to influence policy, intent on deflecting initiatives adverse to their own particular interests, these groups are in a never-ending tug-of-war over education policy. The politics of parochialism prevails. Such was the message of the Public Agenda report.[11] Gridlock wins.

The level of distrust within these school districts was illustrated with startling clarity in one focus group held with teachers. The teachers in that particular school were so worried that any criticisms they made of the school system might leak back to the central office that they insisted the interviewer turn off the tape recorder so that they could deny any statements attributed to them. "The moderator was flabbergasted," says Immerwahr. "Our moderators have conducted focus groups on everything from Medicare reimbursement to the criminal justice system to U.S.-Soviet relations, and we'd never encountered that level of paranoia by so many respondents."

What came through clearly in the study was a sense that although most adults in the schools appear to be genuinely concerned with students' well-being, the "primary goal of the schools—quality education for students—had become peripheral to their day-to-day activity."[12]

Public Agenda's findings make for distressing reading to those of us brought up with a civics book view about how public institutions operate:

—Education stakeholders view each others' motivations in Machiavellian terms. In each of the communities, participants acknowledged that conflict is endemic, that no one seems to be looking out for the common good, and that the logic of school system organization compels groups to act on partisan interests for fear of having to shoulder unfair burdens if they do not.

—In all four communities the majority of stakeholders concluded that the best way to achieve their goals was to band together with allies and press their special interest or concern. So parental protests can restore a teaching position or keep a school open; threats of lawsuits by interest groups can reinstate suspended students; and union muscle can protect teachers' pay and even the jobs of incompetent teachers.

—Parents get into the act too, but as activists on behalf of their own children, not as advocates for all children. The squeaky wheel gets greased, and activist parents have learned how to make the system work for them, although, ironically, the school systems' responsiveness to activist parents works to maintain the status quo for everyone else.

—The veil of politics obscuring relationships within the districts leaves respondents of all kinds, including parents, teachers, and administrators, afraid and intimidated.

—Surviving amid these politics requires the skills of a peace negotiator in the Middle East or Belfast. Superintendents try to stitch together patchwork alliances of partisan groups and reach compromises over management and policy issues. "I'm like a shuttle diplomat," one superintendent said.

—Past reform efforts have left a legacy of skepticism and suspicion in their wake. All the actors have become accustomed to reforms and to changes in key players. Cynicism often greets the latest "reform du jour."

Leaders of the total quality management effort in business like to speak of "constancy of purpose" as an important part of the quality culture. By that they mean that everyone in the organization needs not only to share the same vision of what they are trying to accomplish but also to maintain that vision despite the temptation to wander off in different directions. Far from sharing the same vision, some of the people running and staffing American schools are barely on speaking terms.

Why Change Is So Tough

Given all these factors—inherited attitudes, the emphasis on process, sheer inertia, and the warring camps inside and outside the schools— it is no wonder reform is so hard. Change is difficult to begin with. The existing system serves the needs of adults within the system pretty well. All the participants in this complex calculus have every self-interest in the world arguing against reform. Only the public interest argues in favor of it.

Owen "Brad" Butler was for many years head of the consumer products giant Procter & Gamble. Butler was also deeply, personally committed to American education as the foundation of individual and national welfare. As a member of the Committee for Economic Development, a coalition of business and university CEOs, he helped develop two important statements that, in essence, called on American voters and public officials to consider preschool programs and support for education as "investments" in the American future.

Butler also served as a mentor to many business leaders interested in education. He liked to remind us of how hard it was to change corporate culture.[13] Every business leader knows from experience, Butler would argue, that changing a $10 billion corporation, employing maybe 100,000 people with a couple of hundred offices and plants and perhaps four union contracts, takes a decade or more. Then he'd lower the boom. "That's mere child's play compared to the task of changing public schools," he would say. "Think about it. Public education is a $200 billion enterprise, divided into fifty totally autonomous divisions, with several million employees in 15,000 subsidiaries, each with its own board of directors, its own CEO, its own traditions, and maybe ten or fifteen different labor agreements."

Butler had a good point. Considered simply as a management proposition, the challenge of changing American public schools is formidable, involving about 50 million students, teachers, and administrators. It is not a task for the faint of heart. It will not be accomplished overnight. But these schools will not be changed if we just continue to wring our hands about the problems. They will be changed when we decide to act.

The good news is we do not need to reinvent the wheel. We can learn a lot just by looking at how other great American enterprises—the U.S. Army and great corporations, for example—have turned themselves around. Lessons gleaned from their experience can be applied to the schools. Even more can be learned by looking at new kinds of schools already breaking the mold. I had a hand in launching one of the most promising of these efforts, New American Schools. But there are others, too. Both kinds of lessons, corporate and educational, are what the following chapters are all about.

CHAPTER FIVE

Lessons from Other Institutional Turnarounds

DONALD E. PETERSEN was uncharacteristically behind schedule. Just a few minutes late for an early afternoon meeting. Not anything most people would worry about, but unusual enough for the normally punctual head of Ford Motor Company that the people awaiting him noticed. Still, the academic and corporate CEOs gathered in the imposing board room at Ford World Headquarters in Dearborn were not about to complain. They knew it would have been far easier for Petersen to cancel the education meeting he was committed to chairing on behalf of an outfit called the Business–Higher Education Forum than to go ahead with it.

The date was September 29, 1987. Just that morning Henry Ford II had died. The dominant presence at Ford in the decades following World War II, the hard-living autocrat who had made Ford a productive part of the nation's arsenal of democracy, the grandson of the company's founder, and the man who sponsored Petersen up the rungs of the corporate ladder was no longer around to keep his eye on the company bearing his name.

Petersen, known as "Pete" to his friends, finally entered the room. Tall and elegantly dressed, Petersen was lean almost to the point of asceticism and expressionless behind his rim-less eyeglasses, On behalf of his colleagues at the gathering, Frank H. T. Rhodes, president of Cornell University, expressed his regrets about the great loss to the Fords, both the company and the family. Rhodes is the sort of Englishman who strikes Americans speechless with admiration. Picture the classic Oxbridge academic don and there stands Frank Rhodes—tall, aquiline, patrician, slightly stooped from years of lowering his head to fix an intense gaze on his conversational partners. Rhodes is also an academic John Gielgud, capable of mesmerizing audiences with his resonant voice and rich command of the language. People never tire of hearing Rhodes; he is the sort of public speaker most people would listen to happily as he read from the Manhattan telephone directory.

As Rhodes offered the group's condolences to Petersen, the automaker's eyes appeared to glisten behind his shiny glasses. Then he responded, acknowledging that it was a difficult day for the company. He had spent part of the morning on the company's global television system, he said, reassuring employees worldwide that the Ford Motor Company was stable and would go forward. Nevertheless, it was hard on people who had known and worked with the younger Ford, reported Petersen. "Today," he said, "marks the first time in my life with this company that we could not turn for advice in the middle of hard times to Mr. Ford."

Petersen had plenty of experience with hard times at Ford Motor Company. In distress about his own prospects for advancement, he had almost left the company twice, first in 1957 and again in 1974.[1] Although allied with Lee Iacocca on the team that developed the famous Mustang in the 1960s, he knocked around in management for the rest of the decade. That changed when Henry Ford II tapped Iacocca for the president's office, and Petersen, at age forty-three, was named vice president for car planning and research.[2] Throughout the 1970s Petersen, busy with his new responsibilities, had almost no contact with Ford's core business—building and selling cars in the United States. That may have been a good thing, for during that period, the core business was busy disintegrating, circling the drain ever faster as losses mounted.

Then, on March 12, 1980, Petersen was given a single evening to consider a new promotion.[3] Would he assume the Ford presidency?

Henry Ford II was stepping down as chairman, to be replaced by the current president, Philip Caldwell. Petersen, who had once despaired of his prospects at Ford, was to become the number-two man in the world's second-largest automaking company, the odds-on favorite to someday replace Caldwell as chairman.

That is when Petersen's education in the hardest of hard times at Ford Motor Company really began. The company's North American operation was on the ropes. It was not just losing money, or even bleeding pretty badly; it was hemorrhaging. Before Petersen had time to savor his new status, he learned that Ford overall was losing money at incredible rates, about $1 billion annually. "I set a record for a president for first-year losses," Petersen wisecracks now.[4] But nobody in Dearborn was laughing then. All told, the company would lose an unprecedented $3.3 billion in the first three years of Petersen's presidency.

Ford was near death, its very existence at stake. Postwar America is littered with the discarded shells of once-thriving automakers— Packard, Studebaker, and American Motors, the most prominent among them. The idea that Ford might join them in the auto junk-yard was not inconceivable. Some said it was even highly likely. As Petersen liked to recall later, "We had to change; we simply had no other choice."[5]

And change Ford did. By the time Petersen and Rhodes convened their corporate and academic colleagues at Ford World Headquarters in 1987, Petersen and Ford Motor Company were living large and rid-ing high. Both the man and the company were atop an enormous crest of corporate and public approval. Petersen was picking up "exec-utive of the year" citations from industry groups and publications like a high school All-American picking up banquet awards. Ford, which had not outearned General Motors since 1924, earned net profits of $3.3 billion in 1986, handily outdistancing the $2.9 billion GM reported, although Ford was just two-thirds GM's size.[6] The 1986 earnings signaled a remarkable turnaround in which Ford posted one record after another—net income of $4.6 billion in 1987 (the best any auto company had ever recorded); followed in 1988 with the truly astonishing net income of $5.3 billion (the best any manufacturer in any line of work had ever seen).

How had this happened? Who was responsible for this seven-year comeback? What were the secrets of Ford's turnaround? What is the explanation for Petersen's success?

In fact, Ford's recovery from its near-death experience was simply one of the most visible examples of the complete turnaround of several American institutions in the 1980s. Similar stories were being played out across the length and breadth of corporate America. Motorola, Xerox, even a relatively small enterprise like the jam producer, Smucker's, a family-owned business in Ohio, went through the same thing. Before the 1990s were over, Chrysler and General Motors, each a business basket case for much of the 1980s, had also engineered stunning reversals of their own.[7] The Armed Services experienced a similar turnaround; indeed, the U.S. Army transformed itself in the public's mind between the Vietnam debacle and its triumph in Desert Storm. What lay behind all these transformations?

The Common Script

All of these turnarounds, in these diverse settings, conform to a common script, the lessons, if you like, of institutional failure. Because I was a part of one of them, I do not hesitate to use the word "we" in describing the first steps necessary to reverse course. We did not quite go through a "twelve-step" program, but it was pretty close. The fact of the matter is that most of us were in a state of denial about our corporate and institutional health. Many of us were busy prescribing bandages and aspirins for our aches and pains. What we needed was by-pass surgery.

Here, in outline, are the steps we followed to restore our corporate health.

First, we acknowledged that we were skidding uncontrollably toward disaster. We faced up to our denial and looked reality squarely in the face. We recognized that we had forgotten to take first things first.

Second, we admitted that we had ignored quality. Our disregard of quality, based on the belief that neither our employees nor our customers cared about it, was probably the biggest mistake we made. Many of us are still beating ourselves over the head about that today.

Third, we realized that we were out of touch with our customers. We took it for granted they all needed the same thing. In fact, we thought we understood what they needed better than they did themselves. In a way, we took our success as a given. If it ain't broke, we used to tell each other sagely, don't fix it.

Fourth, we remembered one of the important lessons most of us learned in grade school. My third- and fifth-grade teachers in Rochester, New York, Mrs. Maglachin and Mr. Bisco, taught me that teamwork is important. But we did not listen when the best people in our own organizations reminded us that everyone has to work together.

Finally, we acknowledged that we had underestimated the competition. It was only after we had persuaded ourselves that our competitors were not much good—that they were probably just lucky and enjoyed benefits we did not have—that they really started eating us alive.

Each one of the five mistakes that we made is still being made daily in our nation's schools.

And, of course, the secret to the turnaround at Ford, Motorola, Xerox, Smucker's, and the U.S. Army was that when we began paying attention to the business at hand in terms of those five lessons, business took care of itself. Turnaround required five things: look reality in the face, keep your eye on quality, learn from your customers, rely on teamwork, and worry about the competition. Those same five requirements apply to reforming America's schools.

Look Reality in the Face

"Depend upon it, sir," said Samuel Johnson, the famous eighteenth-century developer of the first English dictionary, "when a man knows he is to be hanged in a fortnight, it concentrates his mind wonderfully." For anything short of a hanging, however, most of us are pretty good at denial. We prefer to ignore unpleasant realities. And because we are inclined to explain away difficult facts, by the time we are forced to deal with them, we have to take them up in the shadow of the hangman's noose.

By 1980 the shadow of the noose hung heavily on the U.S. Army and its sister services, the Navy, Air Force, and Marines. They had been so unpopular during the Vietnam War years that young men were fleeing the country to avoid being drafted. Even as late as 1980, with the draft gone, the volunteer Army in place, and the nation at peace, all four services failed to meet their recruitment goals.[8]

In addition to being 17,000 recruits short of its goal, the Army was also dissatisfied with the quality of the recruits it had. Nearly half of these young men and women were high school dropouts and fully 57 percent were minimally qualified on the Armed Forces Qualifying Test. Quite a change from a decade earlier when the draft had ensured a pool of high-quality recruits. What to do in the wake of the Vietnam War and the arrival of the all-volunteer force? The Army had to face reality.

Don Petersen discovered a similar situation when he settled in behind the president's desk at Ford. At Ford, as elsewhere among the Big Three automakers, there were "numbers guys" and "product guys." The numbers guys were descendants of Robert McNamara's "whiz kids"—financial analysts who crunched data and made cold-eyed decisions based on the bottom line. The product guys—engineers, most of them, production specialists, and product developers—were mostly men who had been in love with cars and their mechanics even before they were old enough to drive. Petersen, with an MBA from Stanford, bridged the two worlds. When Petersen and his sidekick, Harold A. "Red" Poling, a numbers guy who would succeed Petersen as president and chairman, got their first look at the books on March 13, 1980, they also got their first inkling of the effects of a decade of denial at Ford. They were shocked.[9] The company's projected revenues were built on a foundation of sand, a corporate fantasy.

"Red and I estimated our projections were based on 600,000 units too many," Petersen told me in 1997. More precisely, the company's financial plans were based on producing many hundreds of thousands more trucks and cars than Ford could conceivably build and sell at a profit. Petersen and Poling ultimately wound up taking about a million cars and trucks out of production.[10]

I received the same shock when I took over at Xerox. I should have been the happiest man on the face of the earth. But a frightening realization began to nag at me—the possibility that Xerox might be close to entering the corporate graveyard. The Japanese were selling products for what it cost us to make them. How bad off were we? We had been sinking for years. If nothing was done to correct things, we were destined to have a fire sale and close down by sometime in the 1990s.

Robert Galvin, president and CEO of Motorola, was worried about pretty much the same thing in the 1970s. Galvin's father, Paul, started what would become Motorola in 1928, when he paid $500 for a little garage shop.[11] By 1996 Motorola was ringing up annual sales of $28 billion. That first shop manufactured "battery eliminators." Those were the days when electricity was transforming urban and rural America, but many families still had battery-powered radios in their houses. The battery eliminator essentially replaced batteries and let people enjoy their radios without having to take the batteries to a local garage for recharging.

Paul Galvin knew when he purchased that little shop that he would be in business for only a year or two unless he found another product. Manufacturers were already putting out radios with battery eliminators built into them. Galvin needed to find a new product.[12] Shortly, the Galvin Manufacturing Company began producing some of the first car radios in the world, the "Motorola," a hybrid name combining motor with part of Victrola (the hand-cranked record players of the era). Today it is one of the largest semiconductor manufacturers in the world and a major producer of high-tech consumer and industrial communications equipment such as cellular phones, two-way radios, beepers, and pagers.

But in the 1970s, Motorola was in trouble.[13] It was running into the same problems Ford and Xerox had experienced, and with the same people, the Japanese. In the late 1960s the company had come out with Quasar TV. It was a marvel of its time, fully transistorized, without a single vacuum tube. Motorola proudly and accurately boasted that if anything went wrong with these televisions, a technician could be in and out of the house in ten minutes to fix it because it carried its "works in a drawer." Many readers over the age of fifty remember the "works-in-a-drawer" ads as brilliant examples of what Madison Avenue was capable of at its best. Within a year, the Japanese came out with a less expensive television. The Japanese ad writers were equally brilliant, proudly boasting that their television would *never need service.* Most galling of all, the boast was reasonably accurate.

On another front, Motorola battled furiously with Texas Instruments throughout the 1970s for the coveted designation of first in the world in manufacturing semiconductors. By 1979 Bob Galvin's firm finally pulled ahead of its Austin rival. That was good enough for third place; two Japanese manufacturers sat in front of them.

Even worse was the dismal realization that the quality of the American products was inferior. Motorola realized it was producing televisions with 164 defects per 100 sets (some sets had no defects; many had more than 1). Japanese sets had fewer than 10 defects per 100 sets.

In 1979 Bob Galvin came to the same realization I reached as I settled in at Xerox. The handwriting was on the wall. "Unless we change what we are doing and how we do it," Galvin told his people and his board, "we'll be out of business by the 1990s."[14]

Lesson Number One from these examples is simple. In a changing environment, leaders cannot afford to kid themselves. That is a sure recipe for failure. They have to look reality square in the face.

Losing Sight of Quality

Ford Motor Company's giant transmission plant in Livonia, Michigan, was, like many other Ford plants in the late 1980s, overrun with visitors seeking the secret of the company's success. The plant, an enormous, sprawling old manufacturing barn of a place, produced about 2 million transmissions a year at the time (virtually every transaxle in a Ford, Lincoln, or Mercury product), and it was run by a veteran from the old school, Gene Wise. A classic auto plant manager, Wise had buzz-cut gray hair, breast pockets brimming with pens sticking out of a plastic shirt-protector, and the look and feel of a man who would not tolerate fools lightly or care for stupid questions.

Probably aware that many of his visitors would not understand what he was talking about anyway, Wise spoke in simple declarative sentences. His visitors were looking for technology, and he was worried about training. They wanted to see environmentally clean rooms, and he wanted to see better control of his inventory. They needed to understand the "secret," and he needed to put out his product. They thought he had a system. What he had was common sense.

"Well, the plant is more automated now than it used to be," he would acknowledge. "Learning on the job is very important. People have to know how to set up the equipment. How to run it. How to fix it if it breaks. We haven't hired anyone with only a high-school degree here in ten years. It takes a lot of skill to work here. Just about all of the people we hire these days are engineers, most with graduate degrees."[15]

Next he would show them the secret. From a drawer in his desk, Wise would withdraw a plastic baggie, just like the ones millions of families use to keep sandwiches fresh. Inside were a handful of metal filings, weighing a minute fraction of an ounce. "We created a new deburring process here," he would announce proudly. "This is the result." His visitors would gaze reverently at the baggie, as they knew they were expected to. But they were confused. Deburring? Metal filings? What on earth was he talking about? Where was the technology?

Then Wise would explain. For years, the Livonia managers had been satisfied that their machining processes were good enough. Then they realized that Japanese transmissions were better seated— the parts fit together better; they were machined more finely. Those differences in machining account for why so many American transmissions tended to clank through the gears, while Japanese transmissions slipped easily through them. As part of Ford's effort to continuously improve its manufacturing processes, Wise's crew had recently developed a new process that helped seat parts of the transmission better. It literally took some of the small metal "burrs," invisible to the naked eye, off what previously had been considered finished gears and gaskets. They were now better polished. The Ford "secret" was not technology, not environmentally clean rooms, not a complicated manufacturing system but the minute improvement contained in the baggie. Ford's secret was to try continually to improve every aspect of its manufacturing processes—the effort is ceaseless, tireless, relentless.

That is what continuous improvement meant on the factory floor. At the level of the corporate boardroom, however, it was cloaked in visionary terms—Total Quality Management, Commitment to Excellence, Preparing for the 21st Century, and the like. At Motorola they refer to the effort to produce virtually defect-free products as Six Sigma.

Don't underestimate how much you can improve, is the advice of Bob Galvin.[16] According to Galvin, most people like to think of improvement on the order of 1–2 percent when what they really should be looking for is a tenfold improvement. Galvin preaches the gospel of setting high expectation levels, never seeking less than a 50 percent improvement in anything, sometimes looking for 100 percent. So even though he did not quite know what it meant or how it would be accomplished, when he went to his board in 1979 to report that Japanese competition was beating Motorola into the ground, he announced a quality goal of improving all Motorola products and services tenfold within five years. At that time Motorola products sometimes had more than 100 defects per hundred units; its goal today is 3.4 defects per million units, and it is already operating at 5.6 per million.

Quantum improvements in the quality of recruitment processes and of the Army itself as an organization also underlay the success of the U.S. Army in turning around its problems. "Be all you can be" became a refrain to quicken the pulse of young men and women who were not quite sure what they wanted to do with their lives when they got out of high school. On-the-job training in leadership techniques, the latest technologies, and a new GI Bill that promised to pay for a college education have enabled the Army to meet its goals with qualified recruits every year since 1980. That is an incredible turnaround from the situation of the 1970s.

Competitive pressures were not a major factor motivating the J. M. Smucker Company to emphasize quality. CEO Tim Smucker told me in 1997 that when the company was founded exactly a century before by his great-grandfather, its philosophy was simple: "When quality comes first (in people and ingredients), sales and earnings growth follows." Still, aware that the 2,000 jobs the firm provides in the United States were at risk in the face of massive global change—along with its market of one-third of all the jams, jellies, and preserves sold in America—Smucker's rededicated itself to quality and to education reform. The great wisdom of Tim Smucker's great-grandfather is still alive and well in the company he created: Quality products will bring quantity customers.

I became a true believer in these ideas about quality during my time at Xerox. Ricoh, our Japanese competitor, started running an ad in the early 1980s that made my blood boil. The ad concluded with a killer line: The only thing that worked well on a Xerox copier, the ad said comically, was the "Call Key Operator" button—the button you pushed when the copier broke down. What infuriated me was that the killer line was uncomfortably close to the truth.

If there was ever a product that symbolized the Xerox of that time, it was the 4000 copier that came out in 1987. A medium-speed, midrange copier designed for moderate-sized companies, it had wonderful potential. It could copy on both sides of a sheet of paper, a first in the copying industry. But it came out about a year sooner than it should have. In some people's minds, it came out a lifetime too soon.

As impressive as it looked, and as promising as it was, the Xerox 4000 never worked properly. The problems began almost as soon as it was turned it on and were as basic as they could get. For example, the very frame of the copier itself was out of square. Even then, I found that hard to believe; today, it simply amazes me. Copier fit is absolutely crucial. If a piece of the frame is off by even a fraction of an inch, that is enough to create serious problems. The components inside did not fit properly; often they had to be crammed together. One of the worst problems was that the toner used in the copier could leak out all over the place. Spilling toner is no way to impress customers. It is pretty filthy stuff to find on office walls and carpets.

The shortcomings went on and on. The machine was unstable and forever jamming. Customers had to keep boxes of bad copies to receive credit against the meter cards used on leased machines, a daily reminder of how annoying the machine was. The copier had never been tested in a humidity test chamber and, sure enough, it seized up when installed anywhere in the South as soon as summer humidity arrived. The truth was that we were shipping a lot of products that were pretty embarrassing.

What corporations and institutions need to remember, says Bob Galvin, is that "although 99 is a pretty good grade in school, it puts most of us out of business."[17] Galvin recalls a fifth-grade teacher telling his class that they would have a test on fractions on Friday. The passing grade, she said, would be 100. "That was a great lesson," chuckles Galvin. "Unfortunately, I forgot it until I was about fifty-five years old."

Getting people to agree on quality as the corporate goal is much easier said than done. Don Petersen and I both found it very hard to get the top people and the middle managers in our companies to take these ideas seriously. Part of our difficulty was unquestionably the mind-set in our companies. Leaders and workers alike were convinced that the companies were world class. Why should they change? The critics did not know what they were talking about.

Xerox's Corporate Management Committee, for example, approved our quality plan, originally called Commitment to Excellence, but I doubt that its members had any idea what they had agreed to. Many of our executives, in fact, thought this quality push was nothing more than some sort of management fantasy, Kearns' folly. An amazing number thought it was a crummy idea, or that I and the others supporting it were just naive. But once I had crossed the bridge in my own mind that Xerox was on its way out of business, I was willing to pursue quality, hammer and tongs.

Don Petersen had a similar experience.[18] He claims that middle management at Ford was the toughest nut to crack on employee involvement and quality, although "our hourly people [line workers] were much more willing to experiment." So Petersen began a practice of insisting that he would not attend any meeting unless it related to quality improvement. "I sent a message. I made a point that any meeting I went to, wherever it was held, had to include quality as the number one agenda item. Nothing else was talked about until we had defined the quality issue we had to deal with." His biggest headache, Petersen reports, "was convincing people that quality improvement reduces costs. It is not a choice between quality and cost, yet that was the attitude I encountered everywhere I went."

Petersen was right. My company, Xerox, got into trouble when its preoccupation with growth led it to believe that quality was an expense. There was no pervasive attitude that the product had to be as good as humanly possible. We did not understand that attention to quality throughout the manufacturing process actually reduced costs. Only when the company's very existence was at risk, and the top management became convinced of the need to change, were we able to understand things differently.

Above all, in the corporate change process, we learned that the major reason we had gotten into trouble was that we had stopped listening. Sometimes the most important thing we did in changing our ways was simply to shut up and listen to our customers and employees.

Learn from Your Customers

Frank Pipp joined Xerox as a manufacturing executive in the summer of 1971 following twenty-two years at Ford. He told me once that he was dumbstruck by the lamentable lack of quality at Xerox when he arrived. And he also told me an anecdote I never forgot about an experience he had at Ford indicating that businesses can never stop learning from their customers.

In the late 1960s Pipp was running a Ford assembly plant in California. It was on the West Coast that the Japanese made their first true penetration into American auto markets, and Pipp was looking at all these little Japanese cars chugging around California years before many people on the East Coast were aware of them. Pipp was a product guy. He knew these were good cars, but he could not persuade the Dearborn brass of that. In fact, many of the top people in Dearborn thought the Japanese cars were a joke, pretend cars that Americans would refuse to buy.

Pipp wasn't laughing. He had bought a Toyota truck and put it up on a hoist to disassemble it to get a feel for how it was made. At that time, it was impossible to assemble an American automobile without using rubber mallets to bang together the parts that did not quite fit properly. The rest of the parts—the ones that came out engineered and manufactured properly—fit together easily. They were known as snap-fit parts. When Pipp's crew finished taking apart and reassembling the Toyota truck, they were speechless. They had not once picked up a mallet. The truck was entirely snap fit. Just to be sure they were not hallucinating, they took it apart and put it back together again. It still amazed them; they had never seen anything like it. The Toyota parts were made to far more exacting dimensions than Ford parts.

Pipp then invited some Dearborn people to California to try to convince them that there was nothing flimsy about the Japanese products. He told them what he had found when his crew took apart and reassembled the Toyota truck and invited the Dearborn executives to look over the truck as it rested on the hoist. Everyone looked up at it. They were all very quiet. Then a division general manager cleared his throat and remarked, "The customer will never notice." And everyone nodded their heads in agreement, "Yeah, yeah, that's right," they said in unison, and trotted off as happy as clams at high tide.

What Frank Pipp was to Ford, a fellow named Alex Mair was to General Motors. Mair began warning GM in the 1970s that it was falling behind Japanese manufacturers.[19] Like Pipp, Mair must have felt like John the Baptist in the desert; people pretty much ignored him initially, even though he had a lot of things to say. One of the simplest to understand was that because GM produced lousy connecting rods and Honda produced good ones, GM's cars were heavier, slower, and could not get out of their own way—all because of the poor quality of four simple metal rods whose only purpose was to connect the pistons in the engine with the crankshaft.[20]

Despite what the Ford manager thought, the customers did notice. They noticed that the "fit and finish" of Japanese automobiles looked pretty good. Somehow, the Japanese cars seemed "tighter." They fit together better. Their engines purred, and their transmissions hummed. Their maintenance needs seemed to be satisfied by changing the oil. They were pretty good cars. Twenty years after Pipp's demonstration, Japanese car makers had gobbled up 25 percent of the American automobile market. Of every four cars sold in America in 1989, one was made by a Japanese manufacturer, either in Japan or the United States. So much for "the customer will never notice."

Rely on Teamwork

Ask any business leader today what is required in today's work force and the answer is sure to include the ability to work well with other people and participate productively in teams.[21] That is certainly what Jim Harvey and I heard when we talked with people such as Bob Galvin, Don Petersen, and Frank Pipp early in 1997 about workplace change. We also heard it from leaders of smaller firms, men such as Tim Smucker and Jack Rennie, the head of Pacer Infotec in Massachusetts, a company specializing in naval navigation systems. Their comments confirmed everything I had learned about teamwork at Xerox.

We called it employee involvement. My predecessor as chairman of Xerox, Peter McColough, got it started in the 1970s after making some trips to try to understand Japanese management practices. He turned to our personnel people and said: "I've seen what the Japanese do with employee participation. The workers really have a lot of say in how the company operates. Get me some of that." Ideas like that were pretty typical of McColough. He thought Xerox had a lot of smart employees, and he was right. "Take off the shackles. Let them go," he would say. "Let them come up with some ideas about what we should do." McColough was light years ahead of his time with his insight about employee participation, but the process dragged until 1979 when he had to tell personnel again to get moving.

Don Petersen had the same outlook. He wrapped it all up in the concept of teamwork, with a heavy dose of professional respect. "I thought we needed to encourage a little more mutual respect," Petersen says now. "I would say: 'Look we have great engineers. They should be; after all, we hired them. We have great product planners; we selected them. We have terrific designers; we trained them. No way someone in management should be second-guessing these people. Let's see what they come up with. They're the experts.'"

What McColough put in place was a terrific help to me as I stumbled around in the early 1980s trying to figure out how to proceed with Xerox's quality problems. He put a Xerox employee named Hal Tragash in charge of looking into employee involvement. Tragash admits now that he didn't have the first clue what employee involvement was all about, but he wisely kept that piece of information to himself and went on a learning trip. He visited places like Lockheed and General Motors to learn about their experiences with "quality circles." He took in some conferences on employee participation. And he recruited a consultant named David Nadler, who was teaching at Columbia University's graduate business school at the time and doing some interesting work on employee involvement at AT&T.

For months, the two of them wandered around the company trying to drum up interest in employee involvement. They had a tough time. Tragash visited a new Cummins Engine plant in Jamestown, New York, which made engine blocks for trucks. A bold experiment in self-management, it was touted as a forerunner of plants of the future. Teams of workers basically ran the place. They fixed the work schedules. They instituted a pay for knowledge system and a safety management team. Tragash was mightily impressed and started badgering Xerox managers to come along with him. He told them he had seen the future and thought it worked. He knew that they had to see it if they were ever to understand it.

But employee involvement was a hard sell. People were stuck in their ways. Maybe he should not have used the line about seeing the future. I remember one Xerox executive collaring me at a cocktail party to complain that Tragash was promulgating communism and he would get the company into a lot of trouble. But Tragash and Nadler persevered. Tragash did manage to penetrate some of the concrete by writing a series of little booklets describing discrete parts of employee involvement, which he sent around Xerox in waves. They defined benchmarking, outlined reward systems, and described the role of the manager. And he conducted several seminars and created some quality facilitators. Except in the manufacturing area, however, the concepts had a tough time catching on. Nonetheless he laid the foundations for what Xerox was later able to do when it got serious about total quality. A company cannot have total quality without a total commitment to teamwork.

Bob Galvin realized that very quickly. He started a major education and training component at Motorola, one that ultimately grew into what today is known as Motorola University. He asked a promising fellow with a background in engineering and sales, Ed Bales, to help get it off the ground. But Bales was reluctant to take it on.[22] Like many operations people, he thought the central office would derail his career, and he was convinced that training was a corporate wasteland. But he became excited about its possibilities as he realized that Galvin was rock-solid in his commitment to training as part of a new way of doing business.

What both Galvin and Bales understood was that a commitment to total quality and employee involvement introduces immediate incompetence across the work force. "People aren't stupid," says Bales today. "But we were asking them to work in dramatically different ways. We insisted on drastic improvements in quality and dedication to teamwork. We wanted to streamline management by making it more horizontal and eliminating bureaucratic layers. And we demanded a commitment to shoving decisionmaking down into the organization along with participative decisionmaking. The trouble is, most people simply don't know how to do that. We had to have Motorola University."

Worry about the Competition

It hardly needs saying at this point, but the final step is to keep a close eye on the competition. This can have a hard-edged connotation to it, but you can always learn a lot.

Of course, you have to identify the right competitors. Whether one is examining past developments at Ford, General Motors, Motorola, or Xerox, a lot of the problems boiled down to the Japanese. Market shares of the American companies tumbled dramatically in the 1970s.

Every year the Japanese appeared to nibble away a few more share points. And yet American companies had a lot of trouble acknowledging that the Japanese were the problem. At Xerox we spent as much time worrying about the incursions into the copier business of domestic competitors like IBM and Kodak as we did about Japanese competitors like Ricoh. Don Petersen tells me that people at Ford were consumed with what was going on over at GM at the very time Honda and Toyota were driving the Big Three into the ground.

The Japanese are now experiencing their own problems. Who knows where the next competitive challenge will arise? Korea, the People's Republic of China, Thailand, India, Brazil, Ukraine—each of these or others might conceivably rise up to become a powerful economy. That might be hard to imagine in the case of some of these nations—about as hard as imagining that the Berlin Wall would come down, or the Soviet Union would simply collapse. One simply never knows.

Keeping your eye on the competition can be fun. People outside business do not always understand this, but a lot of us in corporations are like proud parents. As soon as we think we are pretty good at something, we want everyone to know. We are particular happy to share our successes with people who are not competitors, but sometimes we even share noncritical information with the enemy. That is how we benchmark ourselves.

When Xerox was trying to develop benchmarks for its various processes in the 1980s, the company found itself picking up ideas all over the place. We compared ourselves with our direct competitors of course—Kodak, IBM, Canon, and Ricoh. But we also went elsewhere. As I already mentioned, Cummins Engine was pleased to show us what it was doing with employee participation. We looked to L. L. Bean, the huge mail order distributor in Maine, to assess our progress in inventory control and response time. We went to an outfit called American Hospital Supply because they were very good at moving a lot of little things around the country and to Caterpillar because it had a reputation for moving a lot big things very well. We learned a lot from each of them.

American Express had a terrific reputation in its credit card business for customer service over the telephone. Their telephone operators could take care of practically any problem a customer called with in a minute or two. Xerox had a terrible time with people who called about our bills. Customers might be held on the phone for ten or fifteen minutes while a hapless operator searched for the information. It often turned out that nobody had it, and someone would have to call the customer back. We got a lot of ideas about how to respond from American Express.

The Transition State

One of the main things I learned at Xerox is that radical change in any organization is incredibly painful. In the language of change theorists, we were moving between several different states. There was the present state, which we had really already left by the time I was tapped to head Xerox; the transition state, where the company still is, despite its successes; and the future state, toward which we were moving, but which we could not fully define. The transition state is not a pretty picture. It requires a lot of hard work and it is rarely fun. That is where Xerox was, however, and we had to make the best of it. That is where American public schools are too, and educators will have to make the best of it, as well.

Applying These Other Lessons to Schools

THIS INSTITUTIONAL SCRIPT can be applied almost verbatim to schools. Although few people like to admit it, schools are already moving in fits and starts through the transition period toward a future that has not been fully defined. It is a future that frightens many people. The transition period is not pretty, and it is certainly not much fun; in fact, it involves a lot of pain and turmoil. But if one bears in mind that this is only a transition period, then the transformation that schools must undergo in the years ahead will be much easier to accept.

As the schools move through this transition, I think it is important to note that each element of failure in American business described in chapter 5 can be seen clearly in American public schools. Denial, taking quality for granted, losing touch with the public, the inability to work together in productive teams, and ignoring and underestimating the competition—each of these critical failures cries out for attention in our schools.

Denial

Take denial first, the all too human tendency to want to avoid the unpleasant truth at all costs. It has been apparent for a long time that many public schools are on the brink of collapse. They include practically all of the schools in the nation's biggest cities, where about 30 percent of all children go to school.[1] In these communities even the good news about American schools does not apply.

In urban schools in which half or more of the children are poor, only 23 percent of inner-city fourth graders scored at or above a basic level in 1994 reading tests administered by the National Assessment of Educational Progress. In eighth-grade mathematics a 1996 test reveals a similar story: only 33 percent of city school children in high-poverty schools achieved or exceeded the basic level, compared with 62 percent nationally. But we Americans are so heavily into denial about the true state of affairs that we refuse to look this reality squarely in the eye. Until we do, nothing can really change.

The truth is that inner-city schools have a tough time putting first things first. Learning, high levels of achievement, and demanding standards are secondary issues in many of these communities. The problems students bring with them to school—poverty, inability to speak English, unstable homes, and violence in their communities—compound the education difficulties. In fact, with the tacit endorsement of their communities, sometimes at their insistence, schools have been encouraged to diversify into a truly astonishing variety of nonschool activities, such as extended care and health screening, at a remarkable rate.

Don't get me wrong. Many of these things are important. The larger educational problem is that these things take time. It may be time well spent, but tackling such issues in the schools often diverts attention from the tasks of teaching and learning and frequently embroils schools in controversies better settled elsewhere. And these side issues tempt many school leaders to coast when it comes to the educational achievement of their students. Educators know they can always provide a measure of protection for themselves by pointing to these other difficult and demanding obligations as the explanation for why their students are not doing well.

The time has come to move past the denial stage. Like families experiencing the loss of a loved one, maybe a period of anger and blame has been necessary, but acceptance must come at some point. Let's acknowledge that in many ways many schools are not working. Let's begin by stipulating, specifically, that middle and senior high schools across the board and that urban schools at all grade levels need attention. That admission represents a small but significant step. Then let's figure out what needs to be done to fix them.

Quality

The corporate quality lessons should be applied to the schools as well. Like Ford and Motorola, Xerox and General Motors, the education system lost sight of quality for a long time. It didn't put first things first. School administrators were preoccupied with the "three b's"— buses, budgets, and buildings.[2] The quality of student learning was often an afterthought. The late visionary leader of the one-million-member American Federation of Teachers, Al Shanker, had an interesting way of looking at this. He used to say that he could not imagine a corporation staying in business if 25 percent of its products fell off the assembly line and a lot of the rest of them didn't work very well.[3] He argued that a corporation in such a situation knew it could not improve the situation by running the line longer and faster but would instead need a whole new production process. Shanker certainly knew that children are not "products" on an assembly line. But he was making an important point in an interesting way about expectations for educational performance. Like Shanker, I think it is about time we focused on school quality.

One insight I carried out of Xerox was a pretty clear idea of what quality is. It is excellence, not "goodness." Excellence does not mean that a BMW, Lexus, or Cadillac is better than a Plymouth, Ford, or Chevrolet. It does not mean that a Xerox copier is better than a Ricoh. All of these products can be high quality or full of bugs. Excellence means that the product conforms to requirements. Excellence means that the product meets customer expectations, that it does what it is supposed to do, and it does it well.

Don Petersen understood this difference between excellence and goodness. He sensed that some of the people at Ford were embarrassed by the company's blue-collar heritage.[4] They considered themselves better than that and thought they should be designing luxury cars to compete with BMW. Petersen turned this attitude to his advantage. He asked people to build the best entry-level cars they could. He asked them to accept the challenge of developing the best cars possible for working families who could not afford to take out a new mortgage to get themselves to work during the week and to the church, synagogue, or temple on the weekends. That challenge led to the remarkable success of the Taurus and Sable automobiles, the first indication in a long time that Detroit could leapfrog the Japanese.

Doing what you are supposed to do and doing it well—that is a good definition of quality, one that can serve for schools just as well as it can for cars or copiers.

Getting Back in Touch with the Public

Losing touch with the public is the next challenge for schools to take up. Stop and think about it: professional educators have succeeded in putting a great deal of distance between themselves and the public that supports them. The story of Howard Fuller's experience described earlier is simply an illustration of the degree to which the education establishment has distanced itself from the communities that support the schools. In business jargon I would say that educators have lost touch with their customers.

My father taught me that the public is a business's best index of its success—whether that business is a mom-and-pop grocery store, a company marketing the Todd Protectographic Machine, which my grandfather established, or General Motors.[5] A business—or a school— can never learn too much from the public, and the customers come in all shapes and sizes.

The most desirable customer, of course, is the man or woman who buys the product, uses it contentedly, and returns, happy and smiling, when the time to replace it arrives. Satisfied customers can tell a business a lot, and they need to be asked about the products again and again. What is it about this copier that you liked? Was this computer good value for the money? How long did you intend to hold onto this car and how did it hold up? Any problems of any kind we should know about?

This first kind of customer is a marketing dream. The astute leader does not hesitate to put these customers and their endorsements into ad copy and on television. Anything that can be done to keep the satisfied customer happy is time and effort well spent. Then there is the marketing nightmare, the customer who is never happy, who never stops complaining about the product. The copier kept jamming. The computer did not have the memory it needed to justify the expense. Keeping the car on the road cost more than the monthly payments. Everyone in business has run into these people. They just never stop griping and whining. Believe it or not, they are just as valuable as the happy customers. They continually apply consumer standards of cost, quality, convenience, and value to products on the market, and they provide the benefits of their research absolutely free. Although dealing with them is like enduring a root canal, they are the best market research available to business leaders.

These people show up at the schoolhouse door, too. They are likely to complain about the quality of the English program, the school's athletic teams, the cost of maintaining the schools, or the need for more tutors in mathematics. Most of them complain about a variety of quite different things, and dealing with them is difficult. But these complainers are pure gold for the school leader interested in improving quality.

And then there are the "customers" the business or the school never sees because they have gone elsewhere. They have made a decision that for one reason or another the product is not up to snuff. Perhaps it is too expensive. Maybe they tried one before and did not care for it. Possibly they do not like the hours the store is open or the service provided. Or maybe they are simply unaware that the product exists. But because these no-shows never buy the product, they cannot teach the business anything.

In many ways, what these no-shows have to say about quality is much more valuable than anything that either the happy customer or the complainer has to say, for they represent the line in the sand that a business cannot afford to cross if it hopes to keep the customers it already has. Just as I needed to know why some people liked Ricoh copiers better than Xerox equipment, and Don Petersen needed to know why some people preferred a Chevy or a Toyota to a Ford, public school leaders need to find out why some families in the United States have turned their back on a free public education in favor of paying for a different kind of education at independent and parochial schools. These no-shows should have a great deal to teach the public schools.

I know, just as Al Shanker did, that students and parents are not customers in a market sense. I genuinely believe that it would be inappropriate to think of them that way in a democratic society. Still, there are happy customers, continual complainers, and no-shows in the world of schools, and it is not a bad idea to think about what that means.

First, let's acknowledge the obvious. Just about every high school produces a valedictorian and many other successful young people, who will go on to realize the wonderful things life holds in store for them. These are the happy customers. And we can learn from them. But there are also a lot of perpetual complainers. About one-quarter of all young people leave school without a diploma; they drop off the assembly line, in Shanker's metaphor. College admissions deans and corporate personnel officers fret about the skills of many of those who do graduate from high school. Parents complain that schools are not serious about discipline and the basics.[6] High school students themselves report they would have more respect for their schools if the schools demanded more of them.[7] These complaints must be taken seriously, too.

And, finally, large numbers of potential school "customers" are no-shows. These are families that have chosen, for one reason or another, to send their children to independent schools, often at great expense to themselves. Let's be quite clear about what this choice means. These no-show parents have already paid, through their taxes, for a public education for their child. Whatever their reasons—and whatever their economic status—they have turned their back on that sunk cost and decided to dig into their wallets again. As a businessman, I find that to be a remarkable statement of dissatisfaction. By voting with their pocketbooks as well as their feet, these no-shows are saying that local public schools are not delivering the quality that parents have a right to expect.

All of these customers, but particularly the complainers and the no-shows, should keep school leaders awake at night. The axiom is just as true in the world of schools as it is in the worlds of cars and copiers: The customer always notices. And the customer is always right.

Need for Teamwork

Addressing all of these problems can work together to help turn the schools around, but it is hard for me to imagine that will happen without a renewed commitment to teamwork. Right now, teamwork in most of the public schools is wretched. They are completely dysfunctional organizations.

Ben Canada defined the dilemma well in a 1997 conversation with Jim Harvey. Canada is an experienced and savvy African American educator who knows what he is doing and understands where the bodies are buried. As a young civil rights activist in the South, he remembers a policeman holding a gun to his head. He has served as a school superintendent in Arizona, Georgia, and Mississippi and is currently superintendent of public schools in Portland, Oregon. Sturdily and generously built, not to put too fine a point on it, Canada comes across as rock-solid, the kind of man other people trust.

"As a superintendent, I've come to think of myself as jack-in-the-box," says Canada.[8] He invites his listener to remember the jack-in-the-box toy that just about every child has had at one point or another. Canada hums "Pop Goes the Weasel" under his breath as he imitates a child cranking the toy. "Pop! Out comes Jack!" says Canada. Many children playing with the toy go through the same sequence, he notes. First, they try to speed up the music so that Jack cannot get out. No matter how fast the child goes, it makes no difference. Jack always gets out. Then the child slows down the music, cranking it out note by note to try to sneak past Jack. But every time the music reaches "Pop!" out he comes. Finally, the child starts slapping Jack back into the box every time he shows his face. And if other kids are around, they help out too. Pretty soon, everyone is slapping Jack down.

"Every time anyone tries to change anything in the schools, there's always someone else to slap him down," says Canada. Often people are lined up to see who can stuff change back in the box the fastest. Sometimes it is teachers, sometimes staff; often it is the board; occasionally it is parents or local civic groups.

Getting all of the stakeholders in the schools to agree on how to proceed is a complicated business. It involves teachers and their unions, building principals and district officials, and the public in a variety of guises, including its elected representatives. All of them have to agree on the same change and cooperate in order to achieve it. But any of them individually can veto it. In fact, it is so hard to get everyone singing from the same page at the same time that, for the most part, no one tries any more. School management, overwhelmed by relentless suspicion and mistrust, has come to run on decisions made on the basis of political negotiations.

Taking the Competition for Granted

Probably the biggest mistake that Xerox and other businesses made was to take their competition for granted. We fooled ourselves. We persuaded ourselves that most of our competitors were not very good and succeeded largely through luck. When they began to gain the upper hand, we convinced ourselves that they enjoyed unfair advantages, like government support or closed markets. We were wrong. Most of them were pretty good. They were not beating us because they enjoyed advantages we did not have; they were beating us because we had let them become better than we were.

I think public educators are fooling themselves in precisely the same way. It is true that independent schools have advantages public schools do not have. They have parental choice and the parental involvement that comes with choice. They are generally smaller and educationally more intimate schools and thus better able to know the strengths and needs of students and teachers. There is no reason, however, that public schools could not have all of these things and every reason that they should.

Let's acknowledge that the average student at most independent schools arrives in the morning with advantages denied to many students in public schools, particularly those in low-income urban and rural areas. Many, but by no means all, students in independent schools come from relatively intact, well-functioning families. Violence and drug-dealing are largely unknown in their neighborhoods. And many enjoy the benefits of affluence and middle- or upper-middle-class incomes. Fair enough. Those are distinct benefits enjoyed by the teachers and administrators at many independent schools. Public school leaders have a perfect right to point them out.

But in most inner-city parochial schools, many of the students are identical to their friends attending public schools. Sometimes, a majority of these students are not even Catholic. And here, the evidence is long-standing and clear: low-income, minority students attending these schools, with their rigorous standards for performance and behavior, invariably outperform their peers in public schools.[9] Indeed, the longer one looks at the advantages of parochial and private schools (such as choice and size), the easier it is to see that public schools do not enjoy them precisely because of the choices public educators have made about how to go about their work.

I think that a strong case can be made that it is the public schools that have the unfair advantages. Only public schools enjoy government support. It is only the public schools that can "draft" their enrollment. In just the way the Army used to draft its recruits who had little choice but to comply, only today's public schools can insist that all students within a certain area enroll in a specific program if they want a public education. And only public schools are guaranteed a perpetual existence, regardless of their educational performance. In fact, with a few notable exceptions, the only way a public school in the United States closes is if its physical plant or enrollment base collapses. Other than that, it is business as usual. Each school has a guaranteed market.

In public education, we are kidding ourselves. Private and parochial schools are good. They are not outperforming public schools because they have advantages the public schools do not have; they are beating the public schools because despite the advantages the public schools enjoy, public administrators have allowed the private and parochial schools to become better than the public schools.

The Process of Change

Beyond the lessons of the institutional script for change, I think we learned a great deal at Xerox about what the process of change is all about. Most of those lessons are probably directly applicable to schools as well.

The first lesson is that change is not a one-shot program but a perpetual process, a race really without a finish. Change must be worked on day after day after day, building success on success.

The second lesson is that the quality and change agendas have a human face. On one level that means they involve corporate politics. They involve them not in the negative sense of currying favor with whoever is on first, but in the practical sense of understanding the distribution of power in large complex organizations and what that means if change is to be accomplished. For example, when we initiated our quality revolution at Xerox, we realized that just getting the "six kings" on board, the company's most senior managers, would not achieve our goals. We also needed to work with the "eight princes," the group next in line, if we were to accomplish anything. Then it dawned on us that even all of the kings and all of the princes couldn't put Humpty together again by themselves. We needed to involve the entire organization, from top to bottom. We asked the eight princes to recommend some good people to help get us off the ground and with their help identified the "gang of eleven," a loose group of risk-takers drawn from throughout the company, who would join us in plotting the Xerox revolution. Anyone who has ever tried to change a school or a district understands that organizational political consider-ations such as those underlie every major decision.

On a more significant level, the human face requires that people be treated with dignity. That is really the issue behind a question Don Petersen put to Ford's styling department one day. He asked them if they liked their designs, if they would be proud to have this car parked in their driveways? Watching them shake their heads, he asked them to design automobiles they would be proud to own and drive. The resulting aerodynamic shape of the Taurus transformed automo-tive styling worldwide. That is also what lay behind our insistence at Xerox that everyone, from the corporate officers down to the support staff, should be trained in total quality. And human dignity underlies Motorola's commitment to training as well. If quality is to take root in a company's culture, everyone needs to get their hands on the agenda and their fingerprints on the plans.

The final lesson was that vision is not enough. Corporations—and schools—have to be practical too. Vision is important, but vision that is not grounded in substance invites endless efforts to get the vision just right. Too many visionaries are like the family on vacation that never gets the car out of the driveway because it cannot agree on where to go or how to get there. Sometimes, the driver just has to start the engine and get moving.

CHAPTER SEVEN

The Great Promise of New American Schools

I HAVE ALWAYS BELIEVED in invention and new ways of doing things. It is an attitude that dates back to my first years in business. When I was new at IBM, working in sales and taking a management training program in Sleepy Hollow, New York, I was rooming with a development engineer. One evening I came back to the room grumbling about the lack of speed and reliability of tape drives, and the inability of the engineers to do something about it. My roommate stared at me with a look of total exasperation. "Boy, you guys in sales are all the same," he said. "You remind me of the farmer in 1850. If you asked him what he wanted, he would say he wanted a horse that was half as big and ate half as much and was twice as strong. And we would never have invented a tractor!"

That engineer's face never left my mind's eye. It appeared every time I thought about the importance of innovation, whether in business, in government, or in schools. It popped into view again within days of my agreeing to join the Bush administration as deputy secretary of education.

Origins of America 2000

President Bush announced in December 1990 that he was going to nominate Lamar Alexander for the position of secretary of education; Alexander was confirmed the following spring. I was confirmed as deputy secretary on May 31, 1991.

Before either of us was confirmed, we started planning what would ultimately become America 2000. Alexander thought we could get the basic ideas down quickly, and we did. We began with the six national education goals developed at an "Education Summit" organized by President Bush for the nation's governors in 1989. A key supporter at the Charlottesville summit was a young governor from Arkansas, Bill Clinton. The six national goals set educational achievement standards for various grade levels to meet by the year 2000. These included increasing the high school graduation rate to at least 90 percent and demonstrating competency at specific grade levels in a basic curriculum, including English, history, geography, mathematics, and science (for complete list, see table 10-1).

That's about where things stood in 1991 when Alexander and I entered the picture. The nation had six national goals, but no one had articulated a clear idea about how to attain them. And, as administration appointees, we had a White House eager to redeem the 1988 campaign pledge that George Bush would be an education president, but no sense of how that might be done. Alexander and I had our work cut out for us.

We quickly decided that the national education goals offered a rallying point for moving school reform along. We wanted not only to improve schools but also to change the communities in which they are found. So we began thinking of what came to be called America 2000 very much like a campaign. We wanted to change hearts and minds. America 2000 would emphasize grass roots, rely on field efforts, build public engagement, and raise public awareness.

What we finally brought to President Bush was a nine-year strategy to achieve the six education goals. America 2000 was designed to honor local school control, create partnerships between local government and the private sector, and build on the conviction that improvements in American education should develop community by community.[1]

We described it as four trains leaving the station at the same time on four separate tracks. On track one, we wanted better and more accountable schools and proposed financing one of them, at about $1 million apiece, in each of the 535 congressional districts in the United States. Track two was designed to produce a new generation of American schools, and here we proposed establishing a New American Schools Development Corporation, financed exclusively with private and philanthropic dollars. On track three, we envisioned a nation of students, learning throughout their lives. Track four was designed to encourage communities to use technology to improve learning for children and adults through libraries and community centers.

To push all four trains down the tracks, but particularly to advance tracks three and four, we proposed using telecommunications technologies to organize satellite town meetings around the country. In fact, as many as 2,500 communities ultimately engaged in nationwide local conversations, in places like the local WalMart, on issues such as educational goals or standards in mathematics.

If President Bush bought this proposal, we were in business. If he didn't, it was back to the drawing board. Alexander and I took the America 2000 plan to the White House in a state of high excitement. I remember being quite nervous.

The president met with us in the living quarters on the second floor of the White House. As the meeting began, his chief of staff John Sununu and budget director Richard Darman joined us. Bush listened carefully as we laid out the conceptual underpinnings of America 2000 and described the four tracks. Occasionally, he pursed his lips as he followed our presentation, then nodded to acknowledge that he grasped what we were saying. When Alexander finished his presentation, the president said, "Go ahead, guys. I'm with you." Alexander and I were elated.

With the benefit of hindsight, I should not have been surprised that Bush gave his support so readily. What we brought to the White House that day was a ready-made solution for several problems facing the president and his top aides. Bush wanted to be remembered as an "education president." The America 2000 program combined with the national education goals approved by the governors gave him a solid and credible claim to that mantle. During his campaign he had also stressed the importance of local voluntary action, referring to the "thousand points of light" that brighten communities. To advance volunteerism, he later established a thousand-points-of-light program in the White House. America 2000 built on that theme. Above all, it was a community-based strategy, not just another federal program imposed from Washington, D.C.

The campaign we were describing also redeemed the president's promises at bargain basement prices. It is true we wanted $535 million in the budget (and from Congress) to establish a model school in every congressional district. (Naively we thought that would appeal to both Democrats and Republicans. What we did not anticipate was that politicians on Capitol Hill would find a way to pin a partisan label on the request. Congress never granted the money.) An amount like that, more than half a billion dollars, sounds like a lot of money to most people. It sounds like a lot of money to me. But by the standards of the federal budget, $535 million is small change.[2]

Apart from that request, we did not ask for additional public money. The satellite town meetings and community organizing could rely, for the most part, on volunteers and technologies already in place. The New American Schools Development Corporation (which ultimately became just New American Schools) was to be financed entirely by contributions from the private and philanthropic sectors. It was one of the largest investments of any kind by a single entity, public or private, in research and development in education. Alexander and I thought New American Schools would ultimately require between $150 million and $200 million. By the time Alexander and I first met with President Bush, the business leaders on the NAS board had already made commitments for more than $40 million of that total. In effect, we were launching what would become the most significant private effort ever initiated to reform American schools. It was an incredibly exciting time.

New American Schools: The Design Team Concept

The possibilities in New American Schools fascinated me. In developing new products in the business world, managers almost never rely on a single person or even a single office. It is true that occasionally a single employee or a handful of people will stumble across gold. I am told that an engineer tinkering around in the labs of the Gillette Company in the

1960s stumbled across the double-bladed system that became Trac II. Apple Computers' legendary founders, Stephen Jobs and Steve Wozniak, took the "windows" operating system, which we had developed at the Xerox research center in Palo Alto (Xerox PARC) but did not know how to use, and turned it into the architecture of their phenomenally successful Macintosh computer. But these are exceptions, not the rule.

In general, when a business decides it is time to think about a new product, it puts together a product development or design team, drawing together everyone who needs to be involved. The teams typically include engineers, design specialists, finance and budgeting experts, marketing people, sales and service representatives, customer relations personnel, and others. The basic idea is that everyone involved with the new product needs to be in on the takeoff as well as the landing. The point is to try to eliminate situations in which the engineers call for a cooling fan in the heart of the copier, then find that the designers have not made room for it. Or the engineers and designers create the computer of their dreams, only to find it is over budget. Or the company happily builds a new car, only to find the public will not buy it. No company never wins them all, of course, but it is amazing how long the business world went along developing new products by the relay method—each office passing the baton on to the next—only to find a mess at the end. In today's more competitive environment that way of doing business no longer works.

I wanted to apply the same thinking to education research and development. Convinced that many more models of effective school practice were needed, I thought the best way to develop them was through "design teams" that would pull together all the relevant expertise needed. Although I expected that the "relevant" expertise would vary from team to team, a typical design team, as I envisioned it, might include architects, experts on public finance, child and youth development gurus, educational psychologists, systems analysts, computer experts, curriculum developers, classroom teachers, parents, and principals. If a design team had proposed to include school bus drivers, janitors, and cafeteria workers, I would have cheered them on, because in many schools each of these figures probably sees more students on a daily basis than the school principal.

My sense was that too many school improvement efforts had been conducted sequentially or by the relay method. Researchers simply handed the finished product to the schools. If teachers could not use the curriculum—or would not use it—why was it developed? If parents would not buy the ideas, why keep putting them forward?

The NAS Board

When Alexander and I were developing our proposal for New American Schools, I argued initially that it should be a public-private venture. Then it became apparent that the concept would not fly. Even if the House and Senate approved the proposal, budget considerations were likely to prevent them from funding it anytime soon. We did not want to wait for the millennium. Moreover, a Democratic Congress might appropriate $535 million to launch an outstanding school in every congressional district, but it was unlikely to appropriate five cents for a public-private venture in education—particularly one hatched in a Republican administration and overseen by a board dominated by corporate leaders. If we could not get the money from Congress, we would have to raise it privately.

Alexander and I, along with a group of interested, nongovernmental advisers, put together a powerhouse board of directors and started raising money from it. Without exception, the NAS board members were people who knew how to get things done. Most of them contributed generously, either personally or through their corporate foundations (or both), to the seed capital fund that got New American Schools off the ground and fixed in the educational firmament. The board offered another major advantage. Although the department obviously encouraged business leaders to establish NAS, this new nonprofit entity legally had to be totally independent of the government. Alexander and I could cheer them on, but we were not supposed to run it. The board provided a shield from too much departmental interference.

The initial decision to make the board bipartisan sealed the long-term success of New American Schools. We did not want the program tagged as a "Republican operation." Very few people realized it at the time, but of the people on the board with experience in elective office, Democrats outnumbered Republicans by two to one! Although this bipartisan gesture was ignored at the time, it paid big dividends when the Republican George Bush was replaced by the Democrat Bill Clinton.

Once the board was in place and we had completed some more planning, we issued a request for "dreamers and doers" in all walks of American life to send us their proposals for a new generation of American schools that would bring all students to world-class levels of performance. We thought perhaps 200 individuals and organizations might be interested, and that we might receive 100 proposals or so.

The response was overwhelming. Literally thousands of people were interested in what we were doing and got in touch with us; nearly 700 proposals were submitted by our deadline. Of the 687 we could actually evaluate, some 150 were genuinely promising. The staff and regional reviewers whittled that number down to 60, and then to 30, and presented the board with 13 recommendations for funding, along with 17 alternates. The board decided to fund 11.

Making the Transition

As the Clinton administration moved into town in early 1993, it was clear that new leadership was needed to signal the bipartisan nature of the NAS effort. In 1992 a former Republican governor headed the board of directors. After my resignation as deputy secretary of education following the 1992 presidential election, the NAS board suggested that I would be a good choice to replace him. I had a reasonably good relationship with Bill Clinton, and had even contributed to one of his gubernatorial campaigns. At the same time, Gerry Baliles, the former Democratic Virginia governor who served on the NAS board, stressed to the White House the bipartisan nature of New American Schools and how the effort fit with much of what the Clinton administration hoped to do in education. To our delight, in April of his first year in office, both Clinton and Education Secretary Richard Riley publicly endorsed New American Schools on the same day.

Both men were generous with their kudos. They hailed NAS as a potentially important private-sector contributor to Clinton's own Goals 2000 program. That program, as Secretary Riley described it, provided federal support for state and local education planning related to the governors' national education goals; "top-down support for bottom-up reform" is what he liked to call it.[3] Or as President Clinton put it, Goals 2000 would create the demand for high-performance schools; New American Schools would provide the supply. It was clear that both of them understood the importance of our effort to attain the national education goals. However they said it was fine with me; I liked the way both of them put it.

New American Schools

New American Schools is not a program at all, but a concept, an idea about how to proceed with hands-on, whole school reform. It is a unique reform organization, characterized by a focus on the operational aspects of school and district performance and by choice and variety in the school designs it underwrote and now offers. NAS has national reach and scale and a significant evaluation and dissemination component. In the nine years since NAS began in 1990, we have been able to demonstrate that relatively large numbers of individual schools can improve significantly within a relatively short period of time.

Of the original eleven competition winners, eight survived through a full five-year research and development process. What New American Schools really did was underwrite the development of eight new concepts about how to organize and manage schools. We called them "schools of design" or "whole-school reform" efforts.

Some of these concepts would bring bursts of applause from the most hidebound traditionalist. Others are at the cutting edge. Some are broad conceptual approaches focused on student achievement; others are hands on and "in your face." The initial concepts ranged from support for very straightforward standards-based reform to some fuzzy ideas about community-based education. Each of them started from the premise that all students can reach high standards. From there, the designs are as varied as their creators. As the designs shook down, we found ourselves with eight winners on our hands:

—America's Choice Design Network (Washington, D.C.), once known as the National Alliance for Restructuring Education, incorporates a standards-based curriculum, a process for identifying students who are falling behind and bringing them back to standard, and a planning and management system for making the most efficient use of resources to raise student performance.

—ATLAS Communities (Boston) is a concept that combines the work of several scholars and analysts—Ted Sizer, James Comer,

Howard Gardner, and the Education Development Center—to create a unified, supportive school community of learners from kindergarten through twelfth grade. It is an exciting exploration of basic questions about education and learning, collaborative school governance, social service coordination, and parent involvement.

—Co-NECT Schools (Cambridge, Massachusetts) promises to harness the potential of technology to learning. It uses technology as a tool for learning within a project-based curriculum; students stay with the same teacher for at least two years.

—Expeditionary Learning–Outward Bound (Cambridge) offers a curriculum centered around learning expeditions to develop intellectual and physical skills and character. The design is based on the principles of the Outward Bound program.

—Modern Red Schoolhouse (Nashville) combines traditional education principles with modern instructional methods and technologies. It focuses on providing the fundamentals through individualized instruction and a core curriculum.

—Purpose-Centered Education (New York City) organizes curriculum and instruction around a single purpose each semester to focus learning on student-directed interdisciplinary projects involving the larger community.

—Success for All/Roots and Wings (Baltimore) incorporates intensive reading and math instruction, interdisciplinary science and social studies, early childhood education, and family support services to help all students perform at or above grade level in the first years of elementary school.

—Urban Learning Centers (Los Angeles), a partnership of the school district, teachers union, and the community, attempts to meet the needs of children in low-income urban areas by reorganizing the standard grades into learning communities with connections across grades, strong community support, and high levels of participation.

Although the designs of these eight programs are varied, they share several common characteristics:[4]

—They aim to help all students reach high standards.

—They are comprehensive in approach, addressing all core academic areas and issues of school organization.

—They incorporate research about best practices and are the subject of ongoing evaluation and improvement.

—They provide school faculty and community with a shared vision for the school, a common focus on goals, and an organizing framework to shape and direct the reform effort.

—They provide high-quality professional development for teachers.

—They offer innovative and effective ways to engage parents and community members substantively.

How have these ideas worked? They sound wonderful, but do they make any difference? The results of the first years of implementation are just now coming in, and they are impressive.

First, we have learned something about the process of change.[5] As the national leader in comprehensive school reform, NAS takes its responsibilities for sharing successes and failures very seriously. After three years of development and testing in demonstration schools, RAND reported in an evaluation to NAS that delivering the design to schools on paper was not enough. Without complementary technical assistance for school staff, the designs just sat on shelves. So NAS quickly made a shift away from simply developing designs to providing on-site technical assistance as well.

Another process shift was launched in early 1995, again spurred by RAND. NAS evaluators reported that a design accompanied by assistance was not enough to support sustained, successful implementation and subsequent improvement in student achievement. Schools, not surprisingly, were running into barriers created by school district policies, practices, and procedures. We learned that we needed to start worrying about district issues as well as school-level problems.

Second, we have learned a great deal about the effectiveness of this approach, as we have modified it over the years. Based on several very careful assessments of system impacts, New American Schools has a lot to be proud of. Here are some of the results:[6]

—In Cincinnati virtually every neighborhood school that has been able to improve achievement results significantly has been using an NAS design. In addition, ten of the eleven redesigned schools had fewer suspensions during the first year of implementation; eight of the eleven exceeded the district average on student attendance; and parent involvement increased markedly—by 100 percent in some schools.

—Since 1995, when San Antonio began to implement NAS designs, student achievement has improved 29 percent in mathematics, 15 percent in reading, and 14 percent in writing, as measured by the Texas Assessment of Academic Skills. Equally encouraging, the dropout rate is down 45 percent, and the number of low-performing schools, as measured by the Texas Assessment, has declined from forty-four to two. (Forty-seven percent of San Antonio schools work with NAS designs, and another 3 percent work with other models.)

—An affluent district near Seattle, Northshore, has put NAS designs into all thirty-two of its schools. The results: Northshore far outpaces state averages in student achievement, as measured by the Washington Assessment of Student Learning.

—By 1999 more than 1,500 schools in all fifty states were implementing New American School designs. In ten major school districts, different designs are being tried out by many different schools. Meanwhile, the implementation rate is approaching 50 percent of all schools in several large districts like San Antonio and Memphis. In these districts, reform is reaching a critical mass.

The future of NAS may best be discerned by examining what is happening in Memphis. It is a straw in the wind indicating what can be expected in the years ahead. Memphis schools are led by a dynamic superintendent with a youthful, can-do, spirit. Gerry House is one of the leading educators in the United States, recognized by her peers as national Superintendent of the Year in 1999. An African American who has spent fourteen years as a school superintendent, first in North Carolina and then in Memphis, she is deeply committed to the proposition that all children can learn and that all of them can learn to very high standards.

In 1995 she and her board agreed to become one of the major seedbeds implementing the NAS designs. Memphis schools committed to implementing the designs in at least 30 percent of city schools within five years. That year, 33 out of 126 Memphis schools began implementing school redesign models; 14 more schools joined the list the next year, and were followed by another 26 in 1997. That makes the Memphis total 73 schools; of that total, 50 are using NAS models. (The others are implementing a variety of other well-known models, including the Paideia approach, Accelerated Schools, Arts Integration, Core Knowledge, and Multiple Intelligences.)

The gamble of Gerry House and her board appears to be paying off in a big way. In May 1998 the first assessment results of the effort in Memphis were reported. A team of outside researchers led by Steven M.

Ross, professor of educational psychology at the University of Memphis, reports that twenty-five elementary schools that began implementing the new designs in 1995–96 showed much larger gains on state tests two years later than did a control group of schools that had not implemented the reform models. These results provide "strong evidence that the redesign initiatives are having a positive impact on student learning," according to Professor Ross, who acknowledges being skeptical about the value of the designs at the outset.[7]

Perhaps even more encouraging, test results published the next year indicate that the trend continues for both the original cohort of schools and the second one. That is, both groups are demonstrating larger gains on state tests than the control schools. "These findings support the district's decision for every school to implement a redesign model next year," House says proudly. I think that is about right. Indeed, these findings support the argument that every school in every district in the country should go through the exercise of redesigning itself periodically. Because that is what it is going to take.

CHAPTER EIGHT

Other Good News about Schools

THE NEW AMERICAN SCHOOLS EFFORT is the beginning
of the answer, but it is not the end of the story. Many other
promising approaches exist as well. In some ways the educational problem is similar to the problem the farmer
described to the encyclopedia salesman: We don't need to
farm twice as well as we do now; we just need to farm half
as well as we already know how. Schools such as Lester Elementary, sitting right in the middle of a housing project
beside a throughway in Memphis, point in the direction of
where education reform needs to go. Run by a "take no
prisoners" African American educator named Patricia
Garrett, Lester is an example of what communities and
educators together can do when they put their minds to it.

The community surrounding Lester lost out when Memphis schools were desegregated in the 1970s. The predomi-
nantly African American student body was bused hither
and yon in pursuit of an elusive equality. All the time, the
community held out hope that its school would reopen.
For fifteen years, Pat Garrett proudly reports, not a window
in the school was broken as it sat vacant awaiting the return
of the neighborhood children.[1] The community's leaders
let it be known that damaging the school was off-limits.

Garrett noticed something when the neighborhood's prayers were answered and the school reopened in the early 1990s. The summer before school started, she worked late every night preparing for the new school year. Outside, men from the project milled around, cooking hot dogs over a barbecue, drinking beer out of paper bags, and playing basketball and softball loudly. Garrett was irritated by the noise and vaguely intimidated by the men, who were always hanging around as she went to her car in the parking lot. No matter what time she left in the evening, there they were. She wondered if they didn't have better ways to spend their time.

One particularly late night as she locked the school after midnight, one of the men called out to her gently: "If you're finished now, Mrs. Garrett, we'll go on home." For the first time, the reality of the situation dawned on her: The men had not just been hanging around. They had been making sure nobody bothered her or did anything else that might threaten the school's reopening.

The minute you walk into Lester Elementary, you know you are in a good school. Good schools are like that. The second you come through the front door, you recognize that you are in a place that has a clear sense of what it stands for and where it wants to go. You do not need a doctorate or any fancy training to recognize them. The odd thing is that no two of them are alike. Lester Elementary knows what it stands for.

Patricia Garrett sits at the heart of it. "We're doing wonderful things here," she says enthusiastically. All of the ministers in the neighborhood but one have moved to the suburbs. They return on Sundays, but apart from that are rarely seen. The school is there every day. "I'm a Dutch Aunt," Garrett says cheerfully. "I tell the parents: 'You must assume the role of parent. You can't expect others to do it for you.' So I expect to be able to take my kids on wonderful experiences. We've taken them to the Space Center in Huntsville, Alabama. We've gone to Niagara Falls. We've visited Epcot Center and Disney World. And we've taken a group to Washington, D.C. I tell the parents: 'Your kids have to go and that means your beer money has to go.'"

Small wonder that as she moves through the halls of her school, every child she passes rushes up to give the principal a hug. And every child is greeted by name. "We've made this entire school into a resource for the children and the families and the neighborhood," she says simply. "We're not a school at all. We're a family resource center. It's the right thing to do." People like Patricia Garrett are like the engineer I ran into as a young salesman at IBM. They are inventing new educational tractors. The tractor Garrett happens to have hitched her school to is a new school design. She is a big believer in moving ahead. And when offered the opportunity to choose a school design as part of Memphis's commitment to NAS and to variety in schools of design, Garrett did not hesitate to select Henry Levin's Accelerated School model.

Although NAS is the largest and, I think, the most promising of the new design efforts, many different models are under development—Accelerated Schools, charter schools, the Coalition for Essential Schools, Core Knowledge schools, the Edison Project, School Development Program, and Success for All, to name just a few. Even entire states such as Kentucky, Maryland, and Washington are pushing the reform envelope. Consider some of the many ways innovators across the United States are trying to create new educational tractors.

Accelerated Schools

Henry Levin, the former director of the Center for Educational Research at Stanford and now at Teachers College, is a man on a mission. His goal: to create schools in which "at-risk" children are accorded the same opportunities and expectations as what we want for all other children. "Ask yourself the question," says Levin, "Is this the kind of school I would send my own child to?" He calls the schools he wants to create "accelerated schools" because they are designed to speed up learning.[2] To date, he has created more than 900 of them in four-fifths of the states.[3]

In doing so, he has had to ward off superintendents, school boards, and politicians who want to sign up for the benefits but show precious little sign of understanding the difficulty of transforming a school (or a district) along the lines of the three deceptively simple principles that undergird accelerated schools: unity of purpose; empowerment coupled with responsibility; and building on strengths.

As Levin explains it, children have come perilously close to being made "villains" in their own education.[4] Children, rather than the system, are blamed for their educational failure. With the tacit approval of the greater community, educators then set in motion a series of bureaucratic steps to "rehabilitate" the villain. For example, they might stigmatize a child by labeling her a slow learner or remedial student and then slow the pace of instruction so that the child has to crawl even though she can walk. Similarly, schools might smother the love of learning children bring to school by insisting on joyless "drill and kill" exercises. Or the school system might not set any educational goals for students and then accuse them of "acting out" when they become frustrated. Other steps include keeping parents away from the school and making sure that key decisions in designing educational programs are made as far away from the classroom and school as possible. A common tactic is to allow such decisions to be made by state and federal officials and by textbook publishers. Levin and his partners in the participating schools have set out to change traditional mind-sets by establishing high expectations for all students, making learning an exciting and enjoyable experience for children, and engaging the entire school community—students, parents, teachers, administrators, and neighborhood leaders—in the process.

Levin describes the process as "low-budget education reform." The results are as varied as the schools in which they are found. Daniel Webster Elementary School in San Francisco went from near the bottom of the city's schools in test scores to the upper third. Students and teachers in Aurora, Illinois, transformed the gymnasium at McCleery Elementary School into a western desert, complete with cactus, mountain flowers, paper owls, and Native American art. At John Muir Elementary in California, some students learned cooking and gardening from community volunteers who set out to introduce students who disliked traditional science to the value of plants. As Henry Levin never tires of preaching, accelerated school programs are likely to produce very powerful learning.

Charter Schools

Charter schools are not a model at all, but a movement. They are an effort to create innovative, alternative schools, free of most of the red tape enmeshing public schools. The concept is only about five years old, but already dozens of states have authorized hundreds of charter schools in an effort to encourage innovation and improve student achievement.

Charter schools were created out of the reality that individual public schools today have no legal standing on their own; they are simply extensions of the local education agency or school district. Charters change that. Just as individual colleges and universities operate with a charter from the state, charter schools operate with a charter from the state or the local education agency. The terms of these charters vary, but they normally give these schools independent legal standing and the authority to make their own decisions about such matters as curriculum, instructional approaches, and staffing.

In fact, state laws authorizing charter schools vary across the board. Some legislatures have been reasonably generous in authorizing broad authority to create charter schools; others have restricted the concept to as few as ten in a state. Some states make local education agencies the sole source of a charter for a school; others permit state agencies, and even colleges and universities to establish charters.

Early analyses of the accomplishments of charter schools make it clear that the movement is still in its infancy and that a major gap in the information base is how well students in charter schools are learning and whether or not their performance will surpass that of children enrolled in more conventional schools.[5]

Still, the evidence is clear that charter schools have a dynamism that is hard to find in more traditional schools.[6] Administrators and teachers in charter schools are excited about what they are doing. Parents appear to be very satisfied. Enrollment is diverse, with large numbers of minority parents seeking out charter schools as educational alternatives for their children. In one major study involving forty-three charter schools in seven states, nearly two-thirds of the enrollment of 8,400 students were members of minority groups.[7] These schools result from the disparate visions of many parents, professionals from outside education, and community organizations concerned with students' welfare. Many of the students enrolled in them were unhappy or unsuccessful in other schools and are beginning to turn their lives around in the charter school environment. Said one Arizona parent about her child's charter school: "I had to quit my job to drive him to school, but it has been worth it. The teachers never leave the kids alone. They walk with them, eat with them, have longer days, and show a lot of extra commitment."[8]

It seems equally clear that charter schools face many hurdles, according to the reviews. Teachers' unions are often hostile to the charter concept. Administrators often tie up these schools with the red tape they were supposed to put aside. Start-up problems are numerous—from lack of transportation support from the central office to the need to find start-up capital for buildings and equipment. Still, within a few short years, charter schools have become a vibrant force in American education, and parents and many educators are attracted by their humane size and intimate scale, clear and focused mission, freedom from excessive regulation, and the opportunity for parental choice.

Core Knowledge Schools

E. D. Hirsch Jr. has been hurling thunderbolts at the education establishment from his perch at the University of Virginia for several years. The gist of his argument is that traditional educators have abandoned the effort to teach a common core of knowledge and skills, and the concepts underlying them, to all students.

The heart of the Core Knowledge approach is laid out in a series of books with titles such as *What Your First-Grader Needs to Know*. In fact, Core Knowledge is more like a curriculum framework than it is a whole-school reform effort. Nevertheless, many parents and educators find it attractive because it encourages specificity in curriculum; incorporates a great deal of information, ranging from classical curricula and ancient civilizations to Japanese haiku and twentieth-century Harlem; and provides teachers with some ideas about how to teach various topics. It is thought to be used by about 350 schools in some forty states.[9]

School Development Program

James Comer, a pioneering African American psychologist at Yale University, has created the School Development Program (SDP), which aims at comprehensive reform for elementary and middle schools.[10] Its mission is to extend a planning process intended to improve student achievement into the community with the goal of building a common sense of purpose and ownership among school staff, parents, and community leaders.

The program operates through three distinct teams: a school planning and management team (made up of teachers, parents, and administrators) develops a comprehensive school improvement plan;

a mental health team (including school psychologists, counselors, and social workers) concentrates on building positive child development; and a parent program tries to build a sense of community between school staff and parents and draw parents into the school. Together, the three teams try to develop comprehensive plans for school improvement. Originally created to meet the needs of African American children and their families, SDP has also been used in schools attended by large numbers of Latino and white students.

Currently in use in more than 565 schools in twenty-two states, SDP is proudest of the evaluation results originally developed in New Haven, Connecticut, where students from SDP schools showed marked improvement in student performance on standardized tests over a fourteen-year period.

Success for All Children

Like Henry Levin, Robert Slavin of Johns Hopkins University is also a man on a mission. His goal is to develop an educational program for the very earliest years of schooling that will guarantee success for all children—hence the name of the program. "We started out," Slavin says, "by asking ourselves the question, 'If you wanted to change what every teacher does every day in his or her classroom, how would you do that?' Then we asked what elementary schools would look like if we implemented everything we know so that kids never fall behind. Our assignment: Put everything you know that works into a school with high poverty levels and make sure that all children succeed."[11]

Begun in one Baltimore elementary school in 1987, the program can now be found in 450 schools in thirty-one states across the country in urban, rural, and suburban systems and districts. Starting with prekindergarten and first-grade classes, the Johns Hopkins "Success" team will not enter a school unless at least 80 percent of the faculty agrees to try the program. Teachers are asked to "imagine that your job is to make sure that kids coming into kindergarten in your school will succeed forever. What do you do?" The answer includes intensive professional development, early intervention in preschool years, monitoring progress continuously, providing the best instruction, developing back-up strategies such as tutoring for students who need it, developing positive relationships with parents and guardians, and making sure that nonschool services to deal with issues such as health screening, absenteeism, and attendance are in place. "Sometimes that's not enough," concedes Slavin. "So we give one-on-one tutoring, particularly for first graders experiencing difficulty."

When asked what the team has learned so far, Slavin is able to run through a laundry list of transferable learnings. First, he says, a whole-school approach is critical. Reminding me of my time at Xerox, Slavin states flatly: "Training one teacher doesn't work. You have to train all of them." Then he says, teachers have to buy into the new model. "If a super-majority of 80 percent won't go along, neither will we. The dirty little secret of school reform is that principals can kill it or punish innovative teachers. But principals can't balk with an 80 percent majority against them."

Slavin's next point is a policy issue: policy and funding streams need to be consistent. In the current categorical approach to school funding at the state and federal levels, "we need to be able to draw on and coordinate different sources of support to make 'Success' work on a schoolwide basis." The programs must also be evaluated. "We need rigorous, but not complicated, evaluations. Compare your kids with a control group. Involve an external evaluator. And evaluate it more than once. That's all you need," Slavin says.

Finally, Slavin points to perhaps the most critical issue of all in making reform long-lasting and widespread. Scale-up—bringing reform "to scale" so that it reaches more schools and students—requires affiliating with what he calls an educational "religion." As Slavin explains it, innovative schools "need external networks of professional colleagues who are taking the same risks if they are to succeed. These networks are very powerful. Whether it's our group, or Comer's, or the New American Schools, or Ted Sizer's coalition, participating schools need such an affiliation. They get a lot from it. They're proud of the association, they benefit from newsletters and the like, and these networks help sustain the program when initial funding dries up."

The Kentucky Reform

The good news in school reform is not limited solely to whole-school efforts. Entire states such as Kentucky, Maryland, and Washington have also gotten into the act, frequently with the encouragement of my former colleagues in the Business Roundtable. I want to take up the state role in reform in chapter 10, but right now let's look at Kentucky's experience as a good example of what is involved and how difficult such an effort is to sustain.

John A. ("Eck") Rose does not look like most people's idea of a school reformer. His ruddy complexion and thick stubby hands are a dead giveaway of a life spent out of doors handling equipment and livestock. He speaks the homey and down-to-earth language one would expect from a rancher and auctioneer, which he is. But he also presided over the Kentucky Senate in 1990, when it enacted one of the most ambitious reform movements in the United States, the Kentucky Education Reform Act (KERA). What he helped put in place is a notable example of how reform can work statewide.

The impetus for KERA, Rose says, was a successful judgment for a group of plaintiffs who filed a suit challenging the way the states financed its schools on the grounds of equity and efficiency. "We, the legislature, appealed the decision. We said there was much more wrong with our education system than its financing mechanisms. We prevailed."[12] In 1989, the Supreme Court of Kentucky agreed in *Rose v. The Council for Better Education* that in virtually every category employed to judge educational performance, Kentucky schools ranked at or near the bottom.

At the time wealthy school districts in Kentucky were spending two-and-one-half times as much as the poorest districts on education. The court responded to this spending pattern—fairly typical for most states—by ordering the General Assembly to come up with something better. "But we also got a complete bombshell from the court," Rose noted. "The court ruled that the entire system of common schools in the state was unconstitutional and required a complete restructuring of Kentucky education."

The language of the court's opinion left no room for ambiguity:

> Lest there be any doubt, the result of our decision is that Kentucky's entire system of common schools is unconstitutional. . . . This decision applies to the statutes creating, implementing, and financing the system and to all regulations, etc., pertaining thereto. This decision covers the creation of local school districts, school boards, and the Kentucky Department of Education. . . . It covers school construction and maintenance, teacher certification—the whole gamut of the Kentucky school system.[13]

Complete restructuring meant complete restructuring. The state department of education? Gone. Laws, rules, and regulations? Ancient history. Procedures governing the establishment of local districts and school boards? Out the window. The decision clearly covered the entire ball of wax involving public schools. In a powerful irony, the pronouncement of unconstitutionality meant that Kentucky educators had to get back to the basics in every way imaginable.

Within twelve months of the decision, the General Assembly had complied with the court's directives, enacting perhaps the most sweeping educational reform ever undertaken by a state legislature. Assembly members designed a more equitable state school aid formula and found an additional $1 billion annually to pay for it. They endorsed a new set of educational goals for Kentucky schools and students and directed a revamped state department of education to stop bossing local districts and help them meet the goals. The General Assembly eliminated age-graded classrooms for the first three years of primary school and established an incentive system to help schools do better. These included financial bonuses and threats of dismissal for teachers and also for administrators.

For poverty-stricken communities or those nearly overwhelmed with dysfunctional families and community disintegration, the reform established community-based Family Resource Youth Service Centers to provide services ranging from job training and parenting education to day-care for low-income students and their families. Finally, the individual school, not the student nor the school district, was made the unit of accountability and given the autonomy necessary to get the job done, according to Thomas Boysen, the man brought in to implement the reform as statewide education commissioner.[14] According to Boysen, slightly more than half of the 1,400 schools in the state were put under school-based management early in the reform, with a mandate to get on with the job. This was top-down support (state mandates) for bottom-up reform (school autonomy) with a vengeance.

Has it worked? So far the results look promising. In 1996 the Partnership for Kentucky School Reform, a nonpartisan coalition of business, government, agriculture, labor, and education, assessed the effects of this effort to design a completely new system of public education.[15] Beyond the debate about the specifics of the reform, the group noted, the most significant result was the least noticed. Kentucky had taken a huge risk. In about a year, it replaced an education system that had been declared unconstitutional root to branch with a system that launched the most comprehensive statewide reform ever attempted. It changed its system and it changed it on the fly. "Five years later," the authors concluded, "the reform effort is not only solidly in place, it is, for the most part, delivering what it promised."

The assessment pointed to several key areas in which the reform was delivering solid results:

— The focus on results has produced them. Student achievement in reading, writing, mathematics, science, and social studies increased by 19 percent between 1992 and 1994. Ninety-five percent of all schools raised the level of student academic performance, with 38 percent of all schools and 24 percent of all districts improving enough to earn rewards.

— Momentum was turned around. Education discussions now focus not just on problems but also on solutions.

— Public education in Kentucky is now driven by a strong accountability and assessment system, one firmly grounded on testing, performance assessment, standards, and rewards and sanctions.

— As a result, the reform effort has earned public confidence and educational support. Most school professionals and parents believe Kentucky schools have changed for the better.

— School governance is now a two-way street in which a decentralized system relies on communication both from central administrators and from those active at the point of instruction — teachers, parents, and members of the community.

— A commitment to support professional development has assumed major importance in the state and in the reform effort.

— The basic principles and goals underlying KERA have redefined the "organizational culture" of schools across Kentucky. Accountability for teachers and schools has been accepted by teachers, professionals, and members of the public. The concept of systemic, not piecemeal, change has been accepted. The state bureaucracy has been reduced and reorganized to support reform. The education community has accepted change as not only necessary, but also desirable. And giant strides have been taken in making educational opportunity and education funding more equitable.

Other evaluations have also found a lot to admire in the Kentucky program. Although Boysen moved on after the first several years of implementation, the KERA reforms had by then developed legs. One evaluation of the primary school program in KERA (the first four years of school from kindergarten through third grade) noted that rural schools worked hard to implement its provisions, that changes have persisted over time in classrooms, and that needed changes were made in the nongraded environment for five-year-olds. Moreover, the study found a massive increase in state support over six years for teacher training, a jump from $1 per student in 1990 to $23 per student by 1996.[16]

Eck Rose pauses as he considers what he and his colleagues in the state legislature wrought at the start of the decade. He is worried that the forces of the status quo ante (the old educational guard who controlled the system before the reform) are threatening KERA. "Educational interest groups backed us in 1990 because we were pushing for reform allied with more money. Like all of us, of course, they liked the idea of more money. But inevitably, now that they have the money, many of these same people have convinced themselves that we made a terrible mistake. Maybe we went too far; we didn't need to do all that; perhaps things weren't as bad as they were cracked up to be in the 1980s. People simply find change very hard to accept."

Then Rose sums it all up. "There's a big debate right now about the role of education in our society. Why is this debate important? It's important because society has only one chance to produce a decent citizen. What we are really talking about here is the nature of American life in the years ahead."

Getting the reform approved by the state legislature was tough, he acknowledges when pressed. "Why do it?" he asks. Then this farmer and auctioneer answers his own question. In a precise echo of Patricia Garrett's words in Memphis, he says: "Because it was the right thing to do."

Putting Children First in the State of Washington

Similar considerations drove a major education reform movement in Washington in 1992. The people of Washington "must reshape the state's school system so that it fosters the education of all," declared the Governor's Council on Education Reform and Funding at the time. "We must put children first. All of them can learn. It is time we acted on these beliefs."[17]

Act the state did. Challenging three great myths about school reform—that schools can be improved from the top down, that tinkering at the margins is good enough, and that worrying about means (funding formulas and curriculum requirements) is more important than ends (well-educated graduates)—the governor and state legislature enacted a sweeping reform agenda. The program put in place plans to develop learning standards for students; goals for student learning; assessment based on student performance and mastery; major new professional development opportunities; and significant efforts to encourage school-site planning through the elimination of state red tape and opportunities for schools to receive state planning money.

Enacted relatively recently, the reform is still "under construction." But already some of its major elements are in place. According to a 1999 examination of the reform, the Commission on Student Learning (established by the 1993 statute) has identified what students should know and be able to do to succeed in the new millennium, a new Washington Assessment of School Learning (WASL) has been put in place, and it is already possible to identify how schools whose students do well on these tests differ from schools where students are struggling.[18]

In a nutshell, this study revealed that successful teachers and schools have stopped "doing their own thing" and begun to orient teaching and the curriculum around the standards. Comparing twenty-six schools across the state that significantly improved their WASL results from 1997 to 1998 with nine similar schools where average scores held steady or declined slightly, the researchers concluded that reading and mathematics scores jumped dramatically when the entire school focused on changing teaching mthods to develop core skills. The increases were as high as 390 percent in some low-income elementary schools, according to study directors Robin Lake and Paul Hill.[19]

According to *Seattle Times* reporter Dick Lilly, teachers at the Apollo Elementary School in the Issaquah School District spent the summer and fall of 1997 rethinking curriculum and developing new teaching strategies to help students improve their performance against the new standards.[20] The teachers developed plans for each grade level to beef up the curriculum in reading, writing, and mathematics while helping students develop and explain their problem-solving strategies. Abby Adams, the principal at Apollo, told Lilly that the teachers "were surprised at how much more the students could do [in math] than they ever thought they could."

"Changes in the way the improved schools operated were responsible for the test-score gains," insists Robin Lake, who led the commission study.[21] In the schools that marked time, she notes, principals invariably complained about the difficulties they experienced getting teachers to give up their traditional techniques and teaching units, In the improving schools, principals without exception complimented teachers for their willingness to change their ways.

The lessons in Washington state seem to mirror those in Kentucky, says Paul Hill. Focus on core skills. Set clear standards. Build accountability into the system. Encourage teachers to unite in tackling problems. Provide teachers with the help they need. Turn control of teacher professional development over to individual schools. Last but not least, involve parents.

Sounds just like Xerox to me. Get a clear idea of where you want to go and then turn your people loose to get there.

Top-Down Support for Bottom-Up Reform

What these state models have in common, then, is a combination of top-down support from the state for whole-school reform from the bottom up. The two work hand-in-hand.

The states supply the demand in the form of goals, learning standards, performance, and measures of various kinds to assess student mastery. They also support schools in meeting these demands by providing teacher training, greater school flexibility and autonomy, and school-site planning efforts of various kinds.

The whole-school reform models—whether the New American School designs described in chapter 7 or the models described here—provide the supply. Despite their differences, these models share several things in common. They represent the school-level analog, with their whole-school focus, of the comprehensive reforms more and more states are advancing. They insist on standards. They demonstrate high expectations for student performance. They rely on rigorous assessment. They offer flexibility and options for student learning. And they are willing to be accountable to the public for their performance.

The issue becomes: How can these pockets of excellence in the system and support for reform in many states be turned into a great national effort that brings reform to schools everywhere?

The Politics of Change: Agreeing to Agree

ECK ROSE IS ONE OF THE PEOPLE who knows just how hard it is to do the right thing. After all, despite the clear shortcomings of the state's schools, the Kentucky reform required a decision from the state's highest court before it could be put in place.

I had begun to get an inkling of the challenge even before I joined the U.S. Department of Education. I had been worrying about education reform for several years, and a lot of ideas about school improvement came together for me in 1988 in a volume I coauthored with Denis P. Doyle of the Hudson Institute, titled *Winning the Brain Race.*[1]

How was America going to win the race? Doyle and I proposed a pretty straightforward six-point plan. To create self-governing, productive schools, we supported choice for parents, students, and teachers; school restructuring from the bottom up; enhanced professionalism in teaching; solid academic standards; a core curriculum, including an emphasis on the values of democracy and citizenship; and an increased federal role in research. Many of these recommendations were standard stuff in the education reform discussion, and much of it still needs to be done.

People liked what Doyle and I had to say about restructuring, teaching, standards, curriculum, research, and all the rest. But everything we said about those important topics was drowned out in the cacophony of outrage provoked by our school choice recommendation.

If our experience is any guide, education leaders will line up to shake your hand if you point out that school organization is wretched, that teaching needs to be improved, that standards are nonexistent, that curriculum is vapid, and that most educational research is an intellectual embarrassment. Hardly anyone will have a bad word to say about you. In fact, most will consider you a fine corporate citizen—and a wonderful fellow to boot. And they will be inclined to agree that although others have been saying many of the same things (and indeed have been saying them for years), nobody has ever said them quite as well as you just did. It is all very gratifying. Little in this world rivals the satisfaction that accompanies giving voice to the conventional orthodoxy.

But in my experience, the smiles turned to frowns the minute unconventional common sense entered the discussion. The applause petered out when school choice was brought up. Now suddenly, I was no longer a fine corporate citizen and a wonderful fellow, but a threat to Western civilization and the American way of life. Interestingly, choice is as American as motherhood and apple pie in most situations. We take choice for granted in practically every area of our lives—whether selecting a Chevy or a Ford, chicken or fish, United Methodist or Reformed Lutheran, Dan Rather or Tom Brokaw. But this basic American value is somehow undemocratic when it comes to public schools. Now, the good corporate citizen finds people lining up, not to shake his hand, but to chastise him for improperly introducing market concepts into the semi-sacred realm of the common public school.

Moreover, the people in the schools who can agree on almost nothing else—school board members, superintendents, principals, teachers' union leaders, curriculum developers, and members of the research community—suddenly find they have a great deal in common. They join hands to condemn school choice, in unison and on key, as the beginning of the end of American public education as we know it.

I learned a long time ago that to get ahead one had to have not only a vision, but also street smarts. It is all right to have your head in the clouds if you have your feet on the ground. Most education reformers have yet to learn that lesson. Educational reformers are idealists. It is their most appealing quality. But most do not have the street smarts they need to go with it. The politics of reform consistently chews them up.

The Politics of Reform

Some years ago, the Business–Higher Education Forum analyzed twenty different blue-ribbon reports on education.[2] All told, these reports contained 285 different policy recommendations. Guess what? Very few of these policy prescriptions agreed with each other. Out of all those recommendations, only 9 were supported by five or more of the reports. Seventy percent of the recommendations had only one advocate behind them. As different captains seized the tiller, the ship of reform went around in circles. It is no wonder the public is confused. Even the experts cannot agree.

Although I think there is probably more agreement today among experts than there was ten years ago, disagreement is still the norm. Disagreements among the various reform camps are a real problem, one that is ignored, for the most part. Although the reform movement can point to undeniable successes, it has also divided into several warring tribes, sometimes split by differences of opinion on educational issues, but just as often divided along partisan, ideological, even religious lines.

One reform map, often thought to be a Democratic one, is actually quite bipartisan. It follows a route defined by national content and curriculum standards. Both former president Bush and President Clinton like this map. Another reform map worries that uniform standards will hamstring schools. It outlines a road leading to local control. You'll find former House speaker Newt Gingrich following this route, but it also appeals to many conservative Democrats and to many fundamentalist Christians. Business leaders, like Lou Gerstner of IBM, wring their hands about workplace needs. Meanwhile, many educational theorists such as David Tyack and Ted Sizer insist that the culture of the school and its moral and civic purposes are the critical signposts.

The Clinton administration, with strong support from the business community, has pursued what it calls a "systemic" agenda, that is, an effort to align each element of the policy system—standards, curriculum, accountability, assessment, teacher preparation, professional development, and all the rest—around common goals and expectations at the federal, state, and local levels.

But many people are like Howard Fuller. They insist that the system needs to be torn apart, not aligned. They believe public education should incorporate market-like mechanisms such as charter schools to promote greater diversity in program offerings and more responsiveness to consumer needs. Both conservatives and radicals can be found following this guide.

There is no reason to believe that all these differences cannot be reconciled in some way with a common map. My point is not that these positions are so fundamentally different that no common ground can be found among them. It is that the politics of reform are so contentious in the first place. Each of these camps is intent on winning the argument, not solving the problem.

The important thing to remember is not simply the degree of disagreement. This tremendous energy and these strong differences of opinion also underscore the transition that education and the public schools are going through. Education in this country is moving toward a future that has yet to be fully defined, and the uncertainty frightens many people. But if we can keep in mind that it is a transition, then the transformation we must bring to our schools in the years ahead will be a lot easier to cope with.

Three Big Challenges

As this transition moves forward, it seems to me that three huge problems must be addressed. We are kidding ourselves about school reform unless we are willing to look these challenges right in the eye. The first problem is incoherence. Any objective outsider would have to conclude that the educational system is a mess, an unfocused, chaotic enterprise. Sometimes I think that it is a miracle that the educational system works at all.

The second problem is that the education establishment has hijacked the schools from the public that supports them. Somehow, the bureaucracy has pulled off the feat of convincing both itself and the public that "public education" and "education establishment" are the same thing. The result is a bureaucratic, unresponsive system, incapable of reforming itself because it has closed itself in and walled itself off.

If that seems too extreme a judgment, consider the reactions of two educators to the disappointing TIMSS results described in chapter 2. In the face of the findings that twelfth-grade American students are at the bottom of the international educational barrel in math and science, one school superintendent shrugged it off, saying (inaccurately) that the tests were "comparing apples and oranges. We educate all our kids; those other countries don't." And the executive director emeritus of Phi Delta Kappa, an honorary society for educators, huffed: "Who cares? And so what?"[3]

The final problem is our own apathetic culture. The general public has failed to pay attention. All of us who do not have a direct role in the debate have said the right things, but most of us have done very little to promote excellence in our schools. When progressives made a mockery of standards and the education establishment hijacked the system, the larger culture acquiesced, looked on in silence, and did nothing. In some ways, we have only ourselves to blame for the mess the schools are in.

Incoherence

Even today, after spending more than a decade examining education in United States, I find it hard to believe that no national consensus exists on what high school graduates should know and be able to do. That very statement probably says all that needs to be said about the state of learning in America. It is a damning indictment of a failure of leadership and will on the part of the nation's business, political, and educational leaders.

We cannot define what high school graduates should know or be able to do because we do not have coherent national standards for twelfth-grade student performance. How far along the road to competence should a fourth grader be in arithmetic, reading, American history, or writing, or any other subject, for that matter? You ask that question in vain. Although experts may offer an opinion—and most assessments implicitly incorporate a position—a national consensus on the answer has never been reached. What about an eighth grader?

The same problem presents itself. In the name of local control, we behave as if Montana schools need to teach a different mathematics from that taught in Missouri and as if a high school graduate from Mississippi will never wind up working in Massachusetts.

Lack of uniform standards is just the beginning of the chaotic enterprise that has been allowed to develop in the name of education. Holy wars are fought within communities and the education profession about how to assess student performance. Raging debates about the merits of "norm-referenced" tests versus "criterion-referenced" tests make the eyes of most citizens glaze over. (The former compares students with each other; the latter compares student performance with a standard.) "Paper-and-pencil" tests are supposed to be inferior to "authentic assessments" according to the experts, but very few people understand what is involved with authentic assessment, including some of the people talking about it the most and the loudest. Lacking coherent standards or common reference points for assessment, the educational system is largely unaccountable to anyone.

This lack of standards and accountability explains why almost no one in any community in the United States can say anything with any confidence about the quality of their local schools. As a result, bizarre public opinion poll results indicate that a majority of Americans think their local schools are fine and that the problems lie with everyone else's schools! In reality, few people know what is going on in their local schools, and local educators rarely trouble to fill them in.

The Lake Wobegon Effect

When they do, the results are likely to be misleading. A few years ago, a researcher at the RAND Corporation, Daniel Koretz, startled American parents by reporting that something known as the "Lake Wobegon effect" existed in American schools and communities.[4] The effect was named after the fictional town created in the 1980s by humorist Garrison Keillor. In Keillor's Lake Wobegon, "all of our children are above average." Reviewing state and local test results, Koretz found that exaggeration of scores was commonplace, a result of directing attention away from individual student achievement toward the average scores of schools, districts, and states. All of America's children, apparently, were above average. And yet, national and international assessments demonstrate less than satisfactory performance, to put it as gently as possible.

What was going on here? One thing, undoubtedly, was that teachers were "teaching to the tests," that is, emphasizing the things the tests would cover. Oddly enough, testmakers and evaluators think that is a mortal sin. They purse their lips and shake their heads when they hear about it. I find that a strange attitude. If the tests were any good, one would expect teachers to teach to them. That is what one would want.

I hope it is obvious that I am not advocating cheating or drilling kids on the exact items they will encounter on the next test they take. Sad to say, that happens. But that is not what I am talking about. What I am suggesting is that everyone in the school, from the principal to the teachers, parents, and students, should understand precisely which underlying skills the student is supposed to learn (and be tested on). With that knowledge in hand, teachers, without hesitation, should orient their instruction around these skills. Will such an approach constrict teachers in any way? Why should it, unless the tests are poor ones? "I used to worry about that," says Providence superintendent Diana Lam. "But then I realized there was nothing on the tests that we wouldn't want our kids to know, anyway."

In addition to teaching to the test in the wrong way (that is to say by cheating), I am convinced that something else was going on as well. School authorities bent the meaning of "average" and "above average" beyond all recognition. Holly M. Jones was director of standards at the Council for Basic Education in Washington, D.C., until 1997. CBE is a conservative organization that has stood for a very traditional education for more than twenty-five years. It has the virtue of consistency: It believes that the education that is good enough for the well-to-do is good enough for the poor as well.

Before joining CBE, Jones was an elementary school principal in the West Irondequoit School District in Rochester, New York. She was puzzled when the state reported that 100 percent of the third graders in her school, and in her district, met or exceeded the state's reference point in mathematics. Statewide, the results were almost as good—95 percent met or exceeded the state's requirements. But Jones knew there were problems in her school; she was, after all, the principal. She understood similar problems existed throughout her district, and she was convinced there were problems statewide, as well. What gives? she wanted to know.[5]

It turns out that the state's reference point was fairly modest: twenty-five correct answers out of sixty-five questions. Jones set out to redefine success for her school. She wanted 80 percent of her third graders to score at least fifty-five correct answers on the test. In 1991, 28 percent did so; by 1995, when she left, 92 percent hit the target.

So it can be done. We need accountable schools and districts. Until we have them, the fictional Lake Wobegon and its above-average children will live on in most communities in America.

Teacher Training

Still unconvinced that the system is unfocused and chaotic? What about the findings of a study of teacher quality led by Jim Hunt, the Democratic governor of North Carolina?[6] Teacher preparation programs are shoddy, he concluded; and teacher recruitment is haphazard. It is little wonder that nearly half of all new teachers leave the profession in a few years.

The problems identified by Hunt's commission are hair-raising. Most states underpay teachers and still micromanage them, treating them as semi-skilled workers. Many jurisdictions spend more time and energy developing teacher-proof regulations than preparing teachers capable of top-flight instruction. New teachers are thrown into classrooms to sink or swim; hiring decisions are made centrally, and new teachers can be assigned to schools sight unseen; and when budgets must be cut, mentoring and professional development are often the first items sacrificed.

But the most closely held secret about teacher preparation amounts to a great national disgrace: Roughly one-quarter of newly hired American teachers lack the proper qualifications. The figures are shameful. According to the U.S. Department of Education, 55 percent of history teachers neither "majored" nor "minored" in the subject in college. The corresponding figures are 40 percent for science teachers and slightly more than one-third for math teachers. Think about that. In order to put a warm body in front of students, the educational system seems to be willing to toss just about anyone into a classroom. It is not hard to imagine what the great American humorist Will Rogers would have made of these numbers. "You can't teach what you don't know any more than you can come back from where you ain't been," Rogers once cracked.

Incoherence is a strong word. Is it too strong to apply to the American education system? Look at the following list: Inability to define what graduates should know and be able to do . . . lack of readily understandable standards . . . assessments that indicate all of America's children are "above average" . . . and disgraceful hiring practices for teachers, the most important adults in our schools. Too strong a term? It hardly begins to do justice to the situation.

Bureaucratic, Unresponsive System

The inability of this system to change itself is the second thing that must be acknowledged. The dysfunctional school family described in chapter 4 behaves in peculiar ways. By and large, its behavior is locked into fairly narrow channels by decades of experience. It has become frozen into predictable patterns, many of them governed by the mysterious provisions of the union contract, and by the even more mysterious requirements of what Howard Fuller calls the "contract behind the contract"—a set of written agreements, arbitrations, court rulings, and letters that are rarely made public.[7]

Imagine, just for the sake of argument, that a reform offering increased funding, district decentralization, massive increases in support for professional development, more accountability, and much greater school choice for teachers and students were to be widely implemented in the United States. In theory, everyone stands to gain from such a combination of changes. In practice, probably not much would change.

Among the potential beneficiaries of such a reform are teachers, with more opportunities for professional development and the satisfaction of improved student learning; union stewards, with new professional opportunities for the teachers they represent; principals, with greater autonomy and flexibility; board members, able to concentrate on policy and focus on failing schools; parents, with greater school choice; and business leaders, with access to the graduates of a more productive educational system.

But these potential benefits, which cannot be guaranteed, are accompanied by equally potent potential disadvantages, some of them almost certain to be realized. Teachers would have to learn new skills; they may well lose seniority rights; some might lose their jobs. Union stewards might lose management as an enemy, currently their most convenient whipping boy. School administrators and central office staff would find themselves in new and unfamiliar roles; some might be displaced in order to put more people into the classrooms. School board members, freed of the trivia of day-to-day oversight, would also lose their right to meddle in the management of the schools.

At the same time, superintendents, many of whom now preside over large central office empires, would find their staffs withering away while they are held accountable for system performance. Parents, who until now have been able to rely on the "system" to make decisions for them, would have to face the task of investigating different school offerings and make decisions about the kinds of educational experiences they want for their children. Civic, business, and minority leaders, basking in the opportunity to improve school performance and productivity, may also find themselves involved in noisy and disagreeable disputes as turbulence in the system mounts and some school jobs disappear.

Public officials would not be let off the hook either. At the national level, leaders of all stripes and persuasions would be whipsawed from opposite ends of the political spectrum as they attempt to advance accountability. When members of the Bush administration, including myself, advocated New American Tests as part of America 2000, we were hammered by ideologues on the political left complaining about the unfairness of such testing for minority Americans. It was with sympathy, but also some bemusement, that I watched Richard Riley, President Clinton's excellent secretary of education, go through the same exercise with ideologues on the right. When President Clinton proposed to develop national tests of third-grade reading and eighth-grade math in his 1997 State of the Union Address, his opponents complained about intrusions into local autonomy. Reflecting on this situation, my friend Checker Finn, a big supporter of standards, quipped: "Republicans oppose any proposal with the word 'national' in it. Democrats oppose anything with the word 'standards' in it."

At the local level a different set of political dynamics would come into play. In some communities, elected officials and school board members have become so accustomed to the schools' needs for bus drivers, custodians, teachers' aides, and cafeteria help that they are likely to balk when they find potential sources of patronage drying up. It was not for nothing that Howard Fuller demanded that people stop thinking of the Milwaukee schools as an employment agency and start thinking about what was required to help children learn.

It is easy for reformers to ignore these political considerations, most of them grounded in educational governance. I know it was easy for us in the Bush administration. Because we wanted to do the right thing, we assumed, perhaps naively, that our proposals would just fall into place.

Now I realize that fixing the schools while accepting the existing flawed educational governance system is like trying to stop toner leaking out of the Xerox 4000 by adding another accessory. Document sorters and automatic staplers did nothing about the fundamental problem in the 4000: its frame was out of line. And standards and assessment systems ignore a fundamental problem with the schools: the governance system is left over from the nineteenth century. Until the governance frame is fixed, fiddling with the education components will not lead to much more progress.

An Apathetic Culture

Even if we Americans fix the chaos and gridlock in the schools, it is not clear that the fixes will improve student achievement. We can hope that they do, but there are no guarantees. Some good things undoubtedly will happen. American schools will focus on standards. The general public will become more attuned to expectations. Parents will have access to much more information about the performance of individual schools. But it is not clear that achievement results will change very much. For dramatic improvements, the people in the United States need to take learning seriously.

Two critical issues are at stake here. The first is that until recently experts mistakenly took public acceptance of their ideas for granted. The schools and the children in them have paid mightily for such monumental pride. The experts and the public were talking past each other.

The second is that although the American people generally like the idea of good schools, when push comes to shove, this society tends to be ambivalent about supporting learning. Not only can the practical, can-do spirit of America easily degenerate into anti-intellectualism. Somehow American culture also tends to think that, for young people, many other things are more important than learning.[8]

Talking Past Each Other

When the Public Agenda Foundation first began investigating public attitudes about schools and economic competitiveness in the late 1980s, it quickly discovered that experts from business, government, and education might as well have been speaking a foreign language as far as the average citizen was concerned. The experts and the public were not on the same page.[9]

Despite a leadership consensus on the need for a standards-based reform movement—a consensus to raise expectations, increase course work, assess progress, and develop challenging standards in core subjects like English, math, and science—progress on reform stalled. Across the country reform efforts backed by broad coalitions of education, business, labor, and government leaders fell apart in the face of determined and unexpected opposition from parents and teachers, and often from community and religious groups. Education leaders found they had been blessed (or cursed) with the old Chinese proverb: "May you live in interesting times."

When the American people think about schools, their first priority is not even on the radar screen of most school reformers. Parents and citizens expect schools to put "first things first."[10] And of all the possible first things, number one is the safety of their children. According to numerous public opinion polls, the general public expects schools to start by guaranteeing safety, order, and discipline. "Whether rightly or wrongly," says Public Agenda's John Immerwahr, "citizens are anxious about drugs and violence around the schools, they're worried about discipline, and their attitude appears to be: 'How can you talk to me about raising standards and performance when you can't even maintain order in the classroom or discipline in the school?'"[11]

Echoing Paul Hill's observation of New York students outside the school, Immerwahr said that one father in Philadelphia told him that "Kids are leaving school in the middle of the day to buy things from the store across the street. Don't teachers see these students outside the buildings? Nothing happens. I mean they come and go as they please. I don't want them to run it like a prison, but I think it's a little too lax.'"

The public, with its feet on the ground, understands something that most experts, with their heads in the clouds, have ignored. Safety, order, and discipline are not separate from teaching and learning. Violence, vandalism, and lack of discipline in the school disrupt learning because they reject the norms of the school and its emotional and ethical structure. They shatter the moral and intellectual worlds of too many contemporary public schools, in the words of Gerald Grant.[12] It may be true that schools are among the safest places for young people, but the sort of mayhem and brutality witnessed across the United States at schools such as Columbine High, in Littleton, Colorado, literally destroy the school as a community. Then the question becomes how to put the school back together again.

Good schools put first things first, in the public's mind. Parents entrust their children to these institutions. They do not want them abused, they do not want them frightened, they do not want them threatened or killed.

Indifference to Academic Values

The second challenge is public indifference—perhaps apathy is a more apt term—about learning. Much of the education discussion has a sort of shortsightedness about it, a reform myopia that pretends it can all be done in the classroom. But it is tunnel vision to suggest that support for learning outside the school is not every bit as important as what is going on inside it.

Lamar Alexander tells me he once went to talk to Ross Perot about educational issues and Perot's leadership in educational reform in Texas in the 1980s. Perot headed a civic commission that pushed for more rigorous educational programs. One of its most controversial recommendations was a requirement that has come to be known in many communities as "no pass, no play": Perot's commission recommended that high school athletes, including football players, be barred from playing unless they had a "C" average in their courses. Communities across the state went ballistic. Perot and his colleagues were tampering with sacred values. "Perot told me," Alexander says, "that getting those reforms through the state legislature was one of the hardest, toughest, meanest things he's ever been involved in."

High school and college students in the United States, and often their parents, tend to view education as a means to an end, not the end itself. The material learned is not nearly as important as the credential earned. The credential, not the knowledge it represents, becomes a ticket to the workplace. So working while attending school is much more common in the United States than it is in many other cultures. Personal popularity is more important than grades. And parents, employers, and prospective employers often encourage these attitudes.

Recent analyses indicate some disturbing things about cultural support for learning in America:[13]

—One-third of students believe their parents have no idea of how they are doing in school.

—Only one-fifth of parents consistently attend school programs; two-fifths never do.

—Widespread peer pressure exists in secondary schools to minimize academic achievement, with three to five times as many adolescents reporting that they want to be "jocks," "populars," "partyers," or "druggies" as want to be "brains."

—Secondary students adjust their academic schedules to fit their preferences for work and socializing with friends, exactly the opposite of behavior in many other industrialized countries where school comes first.

Evidence such as this makes it unmistakably clear that, unlike many societies in Asia and Europe, ours is a culture that often does not encourage or sometimes even value learning.

American schools, and the teachers and students in them, are surrounded by a society that says every day, in many different ways, that intellectual effort in schools is not important. Americans love to hear stories about high school and college dropouts making millions. Universities encourage the attitude when they fob off barely literate teachers on the schools. Teachers and administrators display the same attitude when they throw up their hands in the face of student failure. Employers say it when they hire kids without examining high school records. Politicians and community leaders endorse it when they sneer at teachers. Parents acknowledge it when they worry more about their children's popularity than about their learning and insist that they want their kids to be "well rounded." And community leaders and citizens without children compound the problem when they ignore leaking roofs and dangerous boilers, vote down bond issues, and show more interest in the football team than the curriculum.

Time to Change

It is time to change all of this. The education system needs to be made coherent. The experts have a ten dollar phrase for this: "systemic reform." I will settle for a simpler term, straightening it out, by which I mean making sure that everyone is trying to accomplish the same basic goals.

The system must also be returned to the public. We Americans need to take the education system back from the professionals who treat it as their own possession. We need a new definition of what it means to be a public school. In the face of a bureaucratic, unresponsive system, we need to insist on public schools that are relentlessly innovative and then create the conditions under which such schools will be forthcoming. Then, we need to build as much choice into system as we can.

Finally, all of us—parents, citizens, business officials, community and political leaders, and retirees—need to assess our own responsibility for the educational situation in which we find our nation. My generation inherited what was thought to be a pretty decent system of public schools; we are leaving behind us what is considered to be a pretty awful one. Because each of us played a part in creating this state of affairs, all of us have an obligation to help fix it. In fact, if the situation described in this volume does not strike you, the reader, as a problem, it will never get fixed.

What all of this amounts to is that the education establishment and our political leaders must take responsibility for improving student and school performance. They can do so by putting this chaotic system under a microscope, examining its most glaring weaknesses, and making the improvements that have been crying out for attention for far too long.

Systemic reform, to its credit, attempts to do much of that, but it has several weaknesses of its own.[14] The difficulty with systemic reform as its proponents discuss it is that it throttles autonomy at the school-site level. As Ted Sizer, who founded the Coalition for Essential

Schools, told me in late 1997, systemic reform leaves intact one of the last remaining hierarchically arranged organizations in our society. "What we see in systemic reform," said Sizer, "is the last gasp of progressive administration on the part of today's most able administrators. It's the belief that we can organize the elaborate, detailed, administrative structure that created today's school systems into something better. We don't need a better school system. We need something different, a system of schools. That is to say, quite different kinds of schools that are not like peas in pod, but organized differently."[15]

Systemic reform continues to treat individual schools as the lowest-level unit in a food chain that runs from schools, to districts, to states. The school is governed by standards and rules it had done little to create and can do little to change. The whole purpose of systemic reform, by itself, is to treat the school as a franchise of the district and ultimately the state. Any sign of creativity or autonomy on the part of the school is to be taken as an aberration, a fault of some kind that needs to be stamped out.

That approach, however, stifles the initiative of good people, precisely the reverse of what any modern, effective organization would want to achieve. "What I've seen in years of trying to reform secondary schools," says Sizer, "is friends in middle schools and high schools fighting rigid, unstable bureaucracies. Debbie Meier had to deal with nine different chancellors as a school principal in New York City. You can't fix that kind of instability by insisting on structure."

What I am interested in doing is harnessing the direction-seeking and goal-defining aspects of systemic reform to the autonomy and flexibility required by such innovations as New American Schools and the charter school movement. We need both systemic reform and greater choice. Only these promise our society a legacy of learning made up of uniformly high standards and expectations across the United States and new kinds of public schools capable of renewing themselves and offering abundant choices. In fact, to the extent that people want to characterize this legacy of learning as liberal or conservative, I reply that it is both. It is liberal in the sense that it calls unambiguously for uniform standards and systemic reform, normally thought to be positions supported by the education community and liberal elements in both major parties. And it is conservative in the sense that it supports, without hesitation, autonomy, freedom, and choice at the local level, normally thought to be positions supported by critics of public education and by conservative forces in both parties. The novelty of the legacy is that it recognizes that each of these traditions is incomplete in itself and it draws from both of them.

In addition to systemic reform, what I want to do is hardwire innovation into school processes. It is clear to me that school professionals do not have all the answers, Often, they do not even ask the right questions, and frequently they do not want to acknowledge the problems. We do not want today's solution to become tomorrow's gridlock.

Finally, to secure the benefits of these reforms, the entire public and its major institutions must understand that public education is a public responsibility. All of us share that responsibility together. We need to act on that understanding, which is what the final three chapters are all about.

AGENDA FOR CHANGE, PART I:

Straightening Out
the System

IN AUGUST 1994 twenty-four school superintendents, union officials, analysts, business leaders, and academics came together in Seattle to discuss improving American schools. The meeting, financed by the Exxon Foundation, was pulled together at the invitation of my friend Paul Hill, who had moved from the RAND Corporation to the Daniel Evans School of Public Affairs at the University of Washington. Meeting on the shores of Seattle's Lake Union, the group grappled with the challenge of reconciling two disconnected reform strands in American education: systemic school reform on the one hand, and charter, or contract, schools on the other.

As Hill describes it, the views expressed at the meeting just about covered the Lake Union waterfront. Many of the participants had advocated systemic reform for years. They tended to dismiss charter or contract approaches as "silver bullet solutions" that would divert attention from the need for comprehensive attacks on school problems. They thought, and some of them said, that school choice was nothing more than a stalking horse for the privatization and destruction of public schools. Other participants had helped develop either the charter or contract school concepts. They were inclined to believe that systemic reform, attractive in theory, would founder in practice. In their view efforts to impose systemic reform nationwide would require an unlikely "harmonic convergence" of federal, state, and local motivations and incentives. As with so many other meetings on the subject of education reform, participants at this one were unable to bridge their differences.

"We need to find some way to connect these two reform strands," says Hill. "By and large, they have passed each other like ships in the night. Despite its promise, the reform movement may run out of steam because reformers will fall to squabbling among themselves and let the education system off the hook." According to Hill, advocates of systemic reform have done a remarkable job of worrying about the major features of comprehensive reform at each stage of the system down to the school district level. "Systemic reform, however, essentially leaves the basic trappings of school administration and organization in place within school districts," he says. At the same time, he notes, "charter and contract advocates have reversed the process. They have spent a lot of time thinking about freeing schools from regulation, but have given little thought to the traditional meat-and-potatoes of education policy, curriculum, standards, assessment, and so on."[1]

Systemic reform is a comprehensive approach to school improvement that sets out to align all aspects of schooling around national goals combined with standards for school and student performance. Alignment is just a fancy word for straightening out something. It acknowledges that the school governance framework is out of line.

National Goals

Straightening out the system starts with agreeing on the goals. As my friend Lamar Alexander likes to point out: "It's just like the Cheshire Cat said in Alice in Wonderland. If you don't know where you want to go, then any road will take you there." As a nation, however, we have already agreed on where we want to go. Our destination has been defined by the national education goals, first endorsed by the nation's governors in 1989, and then expanded and enacted into federal law in 1994. These eight national goals spell out specific aspirations for American schools, children, and the wider community to reach by the year 2000. The aspirations these goals define are critical. They put the nation on record in favor of results. They establish school safety as an important national objective. They make it clear that school readiness and school completion are critical measures of success. They stand for adult literacy, lifelong learning, and high academic standards and expectations for all students. They support universal teacher training and greater parental involvement and responsibility. Simply as a statement of our hopes for the future, the national education goals represent a coherent framework for reform. (For a complete list, see box 10-1.)

It is easy to dismiss these national education goals as empty soundbites, but they are in fact a statutory representation of the nation's hopes for its educational future. The day before President Bush left for that Charlottesville meeting, a group of us from the Business Roundtable met with him in the White House. We told him the nation's business leaders supported his efforts to define national educational goals. A decade later, American business still supports the effort and so do I. Although Washington greeted the initial development of these goals with a partisan sneer and embroiled them in a political donnybrook before supporting them in 1994, the national educational goals are not partisan. They were not George Bush's goals, and they are not Bill Clinton's. They do not belong to the president or to the governors or to the business community. They belong to the American people. The national goals do not federalize education, nor do they establish a national curriculum or define national standards; states and localities are left to do that. And they do not dictate how much states should spend, how local districts should proceed, or what the textbooks of America should look like. Local autonomy is left in place.

The eight national education goals enacted in 1994 as part of President Clinton's Goals 2000 were expanded slightly from the goals adopted at Charlottesville in 1989. Two new goals were added to encourage teacher training and more parental involvement and responsibility. In addition, the arts were added to the list of essential learning for a well-educated American. On balance, all of these things can be supported and should probably have been included in the original statement.

It may have been silly to put a time limit on the goals. They will

BOX 10-1

National Education Goals

Here, in brief, are the eight National Education Goals as Congress adopted them in 1994:

By the year 2000:

School Readiness: All children in America will start school ready to learn.

School Completion: The high school graduation rate will increase to at least 90 percent.

Student Achievement and Citizenship: American students will leave grades four, eight, and twelve having demonstrated competency in challenging subject matter—including English, mathematics, science, foreign languages, civics and government, economics, arts, history, and geography and prepared for responsible citizenship, further learning, and productive employment.

Mathematics and Science: U.S. students will be first in the world in science and mathematics achievement.

Adult Literacy and Lifelong Learning: Every adult American will be literate and will possess the knowledge and skills necessary to compete in a global economy and exercise the rights and responsibilities of citizenship.

Safe, Disciplined, and Alcohol- and Drug-Free Schools: Every school in America will be free of drugs, violence, and the unauthorized presence of firearms and alcohol and will offer a disciplined environment conducive to learning.

Teacher Education and Professional Development: The nation's teaching force will have access to programs for the continued improvement of their professional skills and the opportunity to acquire the knowledge and skills needed to prepare students for the next century.

Parental Participation: Every school will promote partnerships that will increase parental involvement and participation in promoting the social, emotional, and academic growth of children.

not be achieved by the year 2000, in part because the congressional debate about them set reform back at least five years. But they lie within reach of the children who entered kindergarten in 1997. Those children are members of the high school class of 2010. Maybe we do not owe it to ourselves to achieve those eight goals—although I think we do—but we certainly owe it to those five-year-olds.

Aligning the System to Reach the Goals

As attractive as these eight national goals are, simply reciting them will not bring them within reach. That is just wishful thinking. Just as the New York Mets will not win the World Series just by setting it as a goal, the United States will not attain its national education goals just by legislating them. Reaching any worthwhile goal in life requires effort, hard work, sweat—often tears and initial failure.

Champions of systemic reform have done an excellent job of describing the hard work that lies ahead. In terms of systemic reform, at least nine principles appear to be in play: Mission and values, high expectations for student performance, standards, assessment, accountability, professional development, preschool programs, social services, and technology. The sheer scope of the effort is daunting (see appendix A for a description of each of these nine areas). None of these principles alone is sufficient; it is the synergy of them working together that develops the power for real change. And all of them have to be tackled together if we are to be true to our commitment to the Class of 2010.

It seems to me that these nine principles of systemic reform can be considered in five major groups: mission and values, expectations and standards for student performance, assessment and accountability, teacher training, and accommodating the dynamics of the modern American family.

Mission and Values

Most people think corporations are all about profits. In many ways that is right. But corporations that hope to make a profit—that is, realize their goal—do so on the basis of mission, values, and guiding principles that keep profits in perspective. When Memphis school superintendent Gerry House joined a corporate board, she reports she was surprised to see how much board attention was devoted to discussing performance in light of the corporate mission statement. Don Petersen says that at one point in Ford's comeback, the company began to define itself in terms of "people, products, and profits" and considered the order of that list to be a significant signal to the public of the order of importance the company attached to those three items.

Joseph Chamberlain Wilson, the man who founded the Haloid Company, the predecessor to Xerox, was an unorthodox businessman who cared as much about human values as he did about profits. When he died in 1971 he was carrying a tattered index card in his wallet summarizing his personal goals in life. They included "leadership of a business which brings happiness to its workers, serves well its customers and brings prosperity to its owners." It took another decade before we at Xerox realized that Joe, as he was universally known, had already set out what we were spending months trying to define, our guiding principles.

A similar examination involving mission, values, and guiding principles needs to take place in every school district in the United States. Once they are defined and followed, they will give us the kinds of schools Americans want.

There is little mystery about what makes a good school. In studies, surveys, and focus groups across the country, parents, students, and citizens, without hesitating for a second, are able to define pretty comprehensively what they want in their schools.[2] They want schools in which

— Safety, order, and discipline are provided as a matter of course;

— A strong emphasis exists on the basics of reading, writing, and mathematics;

— Important values such as honesty, responsibility, respecting other people, helping those in need, and keeping your promises (while not making promises that cannot be kept) are transmitted strongly and clearly;

— Teachers understand their students, know their material, and teach it well;

— Children are treated individually, held to high standards, encouraged to stretch themselves academically, and get the help they need if they fall behind;

— Students understand the importance of what they are taught and parents understand what their children are learning in school; and

— School staff and parents are partners, not adversaries, and adults in the school form personal relationships with children and assume responsibility for their learning.

It is easy to understand what most parents want. The hard part is getting it for them. Beginning with essential questions about mission can help, because, in the end, what these parents are talking about is values.

Expectations and Standards

In our agrarian and industrial past, when most Americans worked on farms or in factories, society could live with the consequences of different results for different students. Able students usually could do well in their careers and accomplish a lot. Most others did enough to get by and enjoyed some modest success. Dropouts learned little but could still look forward to productive unskilled and even semi-skilled work. Society can no longer live with these results.

The imperative for high expectations for all runs counter to the beliefs of many citizens. Many educators do not believe in high expectations either. Only a gifted few can learn at high levels, these people like to believe. They assume (even if they do not say so) that most students are mediocre. By definition, they like to point out, at least half are below average,

This attitude is a tough nut to crack. But it is one that is not shared in a lot of places in the world. People in many other cultures do not accept it. And because they don't, their children's performance is much higher. Recall that the average performance of eighth-grade mathematics students in nations such as Japan, Korea, and Singapore matches the performance of the top 10 percent of American students, according to the TIMSS researchers. Unless we are prepared to accept the notion that Asian students are somehow genetically superior to students in the United States, there is no reason that American performance cannot be brought to that level.

But if we do not believe all students can perform and start behaving that way, nothing is going to happen. Low expectations will continue to be a self-fulfilling prophecy. In the school of the future, we must expect that learning, as measured by high standards of student performance—will be the fixed goal for all students. The adjustable resources to help each student reach that goal then become time, curriculum, teacher attention, and special educational services. As Motorola's Bob Galvin likes to say: "Don't underestimate how much you can improve. Set high expectation levels. Never seek less than a 50 percent improvement, and sometimes look for 100 percent."

Once high expectations are in place, it is time to think seriously about academic standards. Standards define the academic material students should know at various ages and grade levels. Basically there are two kinds of standards. The first defines what students should know, by subject area. These are called content standards. Thanks in part to work that Lamar Alexander, Diane Ravitch, and I initiated at the Department of Education, the major disciplines in areas such as English, history and social studies, geography, mathematics, and science have done a reasonably good job of defining content standards for each of their own areas.

The second kind of standard defines what students should be able to do with this content, by age or grade spans. These are called performance standards. When should students be introduced to *See Spot Run, Charlotte's Web, Crime and Punishment,* or *Soul on Ice?* When should we expect them to master addition and subtraction, long division, simultaneous equations, or trigonometry? These are simply examples of the challenging issues confronting educators as they shape performance standards for what students should know and be able to do at different stages of their educational careers.

I am a big believer in the need to establish uniform and high standards for student performance. Without such standards, the other major leg of the reform stool—autonomy for school sites accompanied by greater choice—will lack a common reference point against which to anchor itself.

Assessment and Accountability

Compared with other nations, American methods of assessing how well students are doing are primitive and rudimentary. It is hard to generate much interest in this situation, or even in the subject. Few topics in American education are as dense and boring as "assessment." Most conferences and meetings about it quickly degenerate into impenetrable conversations that circle endlessly around such arcane topics as sampling, statistical methodology, covariate analyses, confidence intervals, and reliability of the raters. Most people greet these discussions with the response they merit, a giant yawn.

And yet this assessment issue is critical to systemic reform. Once content and performance standards have been defined, tests and assessments must be devised to measure whether or not the standards are being met. Such assessments are not yet in place in American schools. In fact, one of the ironies of the school reform movement is a particularly bitter pill for educators: Reformers criticize schools because their graduates perform poorly on standardized tests. Then, as part of the reform movement, these same critics announce that standardized tests are inadequate measures of student learning and that new forms of assessment are needed.

Despite the irony, the critics are correct. Existing assessments just don't cut the mustard. The United States has an assessment system straight out of Jurassic Park. It relies for the most part on multiple-choice, norm-referenced tests, which grade all students on a curve and require many to fail. There is a better way. It is made up of several parts. The most significant revolves around criterion-referenced tests, which assess students not against each other but against their ability to master the material. Another significant part involves maintaining portfolios of student work and developing assessments focused on student performances. Such assessments are difficult to do correctly, and they are expensive. But as a supplement to existing assessments, they are invaluable.

Teacher Training

This nation needs a massive commitment to teacher training. Our commitment to quality at Xerox incorporated two major elements. The first was continuous improvement. We could never have achieved such improvement without the second, a commitment to retrain 100 percent of our work force, from top to bottom, starting with me, the chief executive officer. We followed a strategy of "training the trainers," so that each rung in the corporate ladder, starting with me, took responsibility for training those on the next lower rung. The idea was that if you knew it well enough to teach it, you probably knew it pretty well.

Neither Ford Motor Company nor Motorola, as far as I know, followed a "training the trainer" model. But each of them also committed itself to massive retraining opportunities for the entire work force when they initiated their commitment to total quality. You just can't get there without it.

In fact, we found the old Xerox culture of growth and expansion so deeply ingrained that everyone in the company (except me and hourly workers at the bottom of the skills pecking order) underwent training twice in the course of seven years. I cannot prove it, but I am convinced that is what won Xerox and its subsidiaries two Malcolm Baldrige Awards.

Training, at the level of effort and intensity we insisted on at Xerox, sends two messages. The first is that top management is serious about improving performance. The second? The company has just bet its future on its human assets. The nation needs to send the same messages to its principals and teachers.

Accommodating Today's Families

It has been a long time since American families resembled those depicted on American television in the 1950s in shows such as *Ozzie and Harriet* or *Leave It To Beaver.* Two parents in the house, with one at home while the other worked, was then an efficient way to support and raise children. But time, the economy, demographics, and new conceptions of appropriate roles have changed the typical American family.

That change is why President Bush's school readiness goal was so important. And it is also why Lamar Alexander is always talking about a little school district in Tennessee and the work of its former school superintendent, John Hodge Jones.

Murfreesboro, Tennessee, is a small city located near the Stone River where Union and Confederate armies fought to a bloody standstill in 1864. Jones, the former superintendent, is nobody's idea of a zealot or revolutionary. With his gentle manner and slow Tennessee drawl, it is easy to underestimate him. But in 1990 he realized that day-care had become a critical need in the community. Single-parent and two-income families in the area were increasing, and new hires were streaming toward a Japanese auto plant opening nearby.

His solution was simplicity itself: The Murfreesboro City schools should offer, at cost, an extended day program with academic enrichment (not simply day-care) to parents who sought it. The response was dramatic: When the city schools announced that one elementary school would be open from 6:00 a.m. until 6:00 p.m. with parents paying for the extended-day services, four students showed up. Within two years, public demand had forced the extension of the concept to every elementary school in the city. By 1995, fully half of the city's 5,000 elementary school students could be found in the program on any given day, all on a voluntary basis on the part of parents.

John Hodge Jones was ahead of his time. Given the way Americans talk about these issues, it is something of a shock to learn that the vast majority of children—69 percent—under the age of eighteen still live at home with two parents.[3] Still, life for children is in many ways immeasurably more difficult than it used to be:

—The proportion of children living with both parents has declined from 85 percent in 1970. Eight percent of American children are living with a mother who was never married, and 10 percent with a divorced or widowed mother.[4]

—More than one-fifth (21.8 percent) of all American children live in poverty, including more than four out of ten African American and Hispanic children.[5]

—About 60 million women with children—married, single, widowed, or divorced—are in the work force, a number that will surely grow as recent welfare reform legislation requires welfare recipients, mostly women, to find employment.[6]

—More than 1 million cases of child abuse, physical or medical neglect, sexual abuse or emotional maltreatment are reported annually in the United States.[7]

—More than 20 million children lacked medical insurance at some point between 1992 and 1994, including 2.8 million who were uncovered for all three years.[8]

In 1993 the Danforth Foundation began a modest experiment to encourage seven school districts to work with their most vulnerable children.[9] It encouraged the seven superintendents to pull together teams of people from throughout the community to coordinate services for these children and their families. With Danforth support "we opened a school health clinic for our elementary schools. We found six-year-old kids who had never seen a doctor," reported Roland Chevalier of St. Martin Parish, a dirt-poor community of wilderness swamps and bottom land in the Louisiana bayou. In Memphis, said superintendent Gerry House, the project has improved coordination between public and private day care. In Bozeman, Montana, then-superintendent Paula Butterfield announced that her community put together a directory of services for children and families—the very first time such a thing was available in the city. These examples tell a story the educational policy wonks often miss. Parents immediately understand it: Families need a lot of support outside the school today as their children grow and develop.

Finally, in responding to the needs of today's families, we need to embed computers and other telecommunications technologies in our schools. The use of technology in American life has exploded, affecting every aspect of life from the workplace to the living room. Young people need access to these new technologies and information tools, to computers, computer networks, CD-ROMs, modems, and the emerging information superhighway. These technologies can help tailor instruction to the individual needs of students. They can help Americans create the kinds of learning institutions they have always wanted and needed; technology can help create schools that tailor instruction to the specific, individual needs of each student and that encourage students to learn at their own pace and throughout their lives.

Because computer-based technology is such an important component of the information highway, I have been particularly pleased to follow the progress of the business community in wiring schools and school districts in recent years. It is easy to dismiss such programs as nothing more than stunts. But they remind the American people of how important these new technologies are.

Who Is Responsible for What?

Straightening out the system requires clarifying something else as well. In this new system, realigned around high standards and systemic change, who should be responsible for doing what? Education has often been described as a national interest, a state responsibility, and a local obligation. In light of what I have described as the need for common standards tied to greater school autonomy and more parental choice, what are the appropriate roles at the federal, state, and local levels? How will they change?

My guess is the federal government's role will become less operational and more inspirational. Washington is neither the source of the problems in the nation's schools nor the solution. But that does not mean that the national government has no role.

During the Reagan administration, the National Commission on Excellence endorsed the "bully pulpit" of the national government. It pointed out that only the federal government had the capacity and the authority to keep education on the public's mind as a national issue, to ensure uniform respect for civil rights, and to support long-term national experimentation, research, and data collection. I think that is right. The Bush administration's achievements in defining the initial national education goals and laying out the America 2000 agenda is a good example of what the national government at its best can accomplish—goal-setting, defining the need for national uniform standards and assessments, and advancing experimentation.

Yet the difficulty both the Bush and Clinton administrations experienced putting in place America 2000 and Goals 2000, respectively, indicates that beyond enunciating and providing some seed money for these ideas, the national government's ability to make things happen at the local level is limited. To move this national interest along, states have to shoulder their responsibility.

It seems to me that states will have several major obligations in the new kind of system described here. They will need to create equitable school financing systems; they will be required to develop statewide uniform standards and assessments of the sort already adopted in Kentucky, Maryland, and Washington. They will also need to enact legislation encouraging flexibility and choice at the local level, although a variety of requirements already on the books can continue to serve the public well.

I will come back to this subject in chapter 12, but here I want to stress that it is time the states stood up for fairness in funding. State constitutions may guarantee equitable school funding, and state courts may try to require it, but the country continues to be bedeviled by glaring inequities in expenditures per student. Nobody can expect a system to reform itself in the public interest if the very system itself abuses the public interest by tolerating the kind of unfair and inequitable funding found in many states and even in many school districts. This situation simply must be addressed.

Standards need attention, too. I was frankly surprised at how quickly the consensus in favor of national standards almost disintegrated in the early 1990s. The clear support of most educators and policymakers for standards-based reform ran into a buzz saw of opposition from highly visible and vocal critics. Some of the opposition was led by educators and teachers; much of it was led by special interest groups of various kinds; it was never clear to me how much support any of these people enjoyed.

Be that as it may, public officials backed away from the standards issue because of the controversy. If it had not been for the leadership of IBM president Louis V. Gerstner, Jr., and the business community, a great national opportunity to push for uniform standards would have been lost. Business leaders understood that the ability to read at grade three should mean the same thing in Kansas as in Florida and that quadratic equations have the same solution in California and New York.

Thanks to the insistence of Gerstner and other business leaders, the nation's governors agreed to continue pushing for rigorous standards in 1996. Gerstner and former governor Tommy Thompson of Wisconsin were keys to getting the agreement and then creating a new organization, ACHIEVE, to continue the push for standards-based reform state by state. Governors and state legislators must stand behind that agreement.

I am impressed with how ACHIEVE is developing support for standards. Political posturing aside, a consensus about the need for standards is firming up in the public's mind. The standards will not be federal and they may not even be national, but I think they will be end up being nearly uniform. The state standards under development do not differ a great deal from state to state. ACHIEVE is now posting state standards on the Internet; it is already possible to dial up the ACHIEVE website (www.achieve.org) to find the standards of some forty states.[10] The website permits a comparison of each state's standards with every other state by major curriculum area. An example would be geometry standards for grades six through eight.

Once that work is completed, linking these standards to lesson plans will be fairly straightforward. In fact, the *New York Times* is already listing lesson plans linked to "national" standards on the Internet (www.nytimes.com/learning).[11] Soon anyone who cares— textbook publishers, school districts, state officials, schools, teachers, schools of education, even parents and students—will be able to compare existing curriculum and lessons plans with standards that are comparable from state to state. The standards will not be "national," but a public consensus will coalesce around the importance of standards state-by-state. Once each state's standards are listed on a website, it is just a matter of time until they converge on one another. At that point any PTA president, school board member, local business leader, parent, or citizen can stand up in public and authoritatively question the adequacy of his or her state or local standards.

To set up the conditions under which autonomy and innovation can flourish at the local level, governors and legislators need to revisit the basic framework within their states governing how public education is administered. In this regard, one of the most obvious things they need to do is enact legislation to authorize local education agencies to contract instruction, including the management of whole schools, out to qualified nonprofit groups. State policymakers should also permit publicly supported schools to become independent legal entities responsible for their own income, budgets, and hiring practices. As part of the effort, they should encourage the establishment of schools that are smaller and on a more humane scale by insisting that the mission of state and local education agencies is to maintain "systems of schools," or portfolios of very diverse kinds of schools.

States should also do several other things to encourage local autonomy in return for accountability, including, I think, loosening up state regulations stipulating mandatory attendance ages for students, the number of days and hours schools must be open, and restrictive labor laws requiring school systems, rather than schools, to employ teachers. In addition, a number of other requirements governing important public interests, such as civil rights, health and safety, building integrity, criminal background checks of staff and teachers, and graduation requirements, already apply to independent schools, and they can be applied to the new contract schools proposed in the next chapter as well.

Finally, we come to local education agencies. The proposals in this book will utterly transform the roles and responsibilities of school boards and superintendents. In a phrase, I am asking them to become responsible for ensuring that innovation becomes a way of life in the schools.

Innovation as a Way of Life

Straightening out the system is not enough. It also needs to be opened up. I have become convinced that systemic reform is, in the words of the logician, "necessary but not sufficient." Despite its promise, systemic reform fails to meet the test of placing responsibility and initiative at the school level. Change must be hardwired into this system by all of us insisting on innovation as a way of life, a continuous process that never ends.

Part of the problem in achieving continual innovation is that the devil we know is always better than the one we don't. People may not be fully satisfied with what they have, but they know the system, understand it, and can manipulate it; it thus serves a lot of people pretty well. Practically everyone can find a good reason for maintaining the status quo. Very few people want to change it.

In consequence, much of the reform discussion inevitably becomes insiders' baseball—a conversation involving a group of experts who understood the history of reform, the positions staked out by various actors, and the secret handshakes of the education community. Because of this, and because most members of the public do not pay a great deal of attention to the details of how schools are organized, educators can easily persuade themselves that reforms requiring few major adjustments in the existing order of things, are really quite revolutionary and promising. That is just human nature. Everyone supports the idea of "change" as long as somebody else changes. We are all inclined to be in favor of new ideas, just as long as they do not require us to do anything different. That is as true of the schools in New York City or Palo Alto as it was in the executive suite and the board room of Xerox.

Systemic reform alone is just such a solution. Even if fully implemented, it gives everyone permission to continue what they are already comfortable with. We need to introduce some measure of discomfort into this world. We have to insist on change as a continuous process, by creating a new definition of what it means to be a public school. Enter the concepts of the charter or contract school combined with complete parental choice among competing public school alternatives.

CHAPTER ELEVEN

AGENDA FOR CHANGE, PART II:

Hardwiring Innovation into the System

ALTHOUGH BROAD-SCALE NATIONAL REFORMS such as the Bush administration's America 2000 and the Clinton administration's Goals 2000 were designed explicitly to encourage local demand for better schools, I am convinced that without other changes, these hopes will be disappointed. Systemic reform of the sort advanced by both Bush and Clinton promises what it cannot, by itself, deliver. The numbers guys at Ford Motor Company would be attracted by systemic reform; it appeals to the analytical side in all of us. But Ford's product guys would understand that the systemic approach leaves out the human dimension of the reform equation.

This human dimension is altogether more powerful in a public enterprise such as education than it is in a private manufacturing concern. Systemic efforts promise to transform the education system without disturbing the human dimension in the form of the governance system. That is like promising to transform General Motors while leaving its legendary bureaucracy intact. The promise is easy to make, but it cannot be kept. The system is not at all likely to be transformed by "systemic" agendas. Far more likely is that the system will turn the agenda on its head.

The fundamental problem with both the existing system and the systemic reform agenda is that individual schools will remain in existence no matter how poor their performance. If a school already exists, its continued existence is by and large taken for granted. And unless some extraordinary community or public disgrace forces action, the tenure of principals and teachers is virtually guaranteed as well. Almost never is failure to educate considered to be an extraordinary disgrace. For that matter, it is rarely even considered a minor embarrassment.

Policy and educational leaders appear to be stuck in the way they think about schools and public education. The way it has always been done is assumed to be the only way to do it in the future. What we call "public education" is simply assumed to be made up of the already existing large, bureaucratic organizations, many of them with budgets and staff that rival the size of governments of small states. The total populations of Alaska and Vermont added together are still less than the enrollments in New York City's public schools. But as these systems work with more students—and more diverse students—we behave as though pushing a little more here and trying a little harder there will make it all work a lot better. It won't. After decades of tinkering with a system established in the nineteenth century to govern common schools (primarily through grade eight) in small villages, it is time to realize that the inherited governance system is itself a huge part of the problem.

Focus on Schools, Not Just the System

We also need to recognize one of the ironies of American education. Although the system claims to prize diversity and local control, most of the nation's 87,000 public schools are hard to tell apart. One elementary school is pretty much like another, whether in Florida or Oregon; middle schools in Vermont look very similar to those in New Mexico; and secondary schools, whether in Texas, Wisconsin, or Pennsylvania, distinguish themselves, for the most part, by the quality of the athletic teams they put on the field. We have created a monotonous uniformity in our schools and called it local diversity.

The nation already enjoys a number of options encouraging greater flexibility on a small scale. More than thirty states have authorized nearly 1,000 charter schools in recent years—independent, publicly funded schools free of most local regulations. Several hundred magnet schools are also scattered across the United States, many of them offering special academic courses to encourage student choice and thus advance desegregation. At the same time a variety of "alternative" schools have come on line, many of them designed for students who are frustrated by the tedium and mindlessness associated with many public secondary schools.

Meanwhile, efforts such as New American Schools have made steady progress. John Anderson tells me that by 1999 NAS was in every state and in some 1,500 schools enrolling 350,000 students. Each of these schools is implementing one of the whole-school innovative designs underwritten by NAS. Another 2,000 schools or so are involved in various other school reform networks.

Although educators like to point to all these innovations as evidence that nothing more is needed, all told it adds up to a pretty flimsy reform effort. It is just a drop in the bucket, maybe only 4,000 or 5,000 out of more than 87,000 public schools. No matter how good the ideas, they just have not come to scale. For the most part the innovative school approaches already in place are isolated; they operate over in a corner where they cannot bother anyone. Paul Hill compares them to eighteenth-century Potemkin villages, communities tidied up to reassure the touring Russian czar that everything was fine.[1] The very term *Potemkin village* has come to stand for an imposing facade intended to divert attention from embarrassing facts or shabby conditions. Like Potemkin's towns, these model schools are cited by defenders of the status quo as examples of just how good the existing system really is and how flexible it can truly be. In truth, they are tolerated as deviations from the norm, not as models to be encouraged. In an ideal world, one would expect such schools to be cloned and widely imitated. Instead they are the exception, not the rule.

For the most part that is because educators can enact such innovative measures only through waivers, through revisions to state code and exceptions that permit flexibility. Or educators may, grudgingly, support a limited form of decentralization, perhaps involving magnet schools or specially limited provisions governing a handful of charter schools.

As I have watched the implementation of New American Schools, it has become clear to me that whenever NAS enters a new community, it has to help reinvent the school governance system from scratch. Most of the NAS designs require decisionmaking at the school level. For the most part that runs counter to the ideology, mission, and powers of the school system's central office. Although the NAS designs explicitly depend on minimizing political intrusion and bureaucratic interference, many barriers still stand in their way. New designs often find themselves in conflict with detailed program requirements, extensive regulations on a variety of issues, traditional viewpoints, and provisions of centrally negotiated union contracts. All of these conflicts have to be worked out in tedious detail, normally through waiver procedures.

Even in places such as Memphis and San Antonio, each eager to implement NAS designs in a third of more of their schools, the negotiations required to put the designs in place took almost a year. I have no quarrel with that. Major changes in schools should not be made lightly. My problem is that I always worried about how well the designs would fare in districts without the enthusiastic advocacy of leaders like the excellent superintendents in those districts, Gerry House and Diana Lam.

My anxieties on this score are not altogether groundless. In general, the average tenure of a big-city superintendent these days is about twenty months. Moreover, despite Superintendent Lam's phenomenal success in improving school performance, the San Antonio school board decided to buy out her contract late in 1998, leading her to seek and accept the superintendent's job in Providence, Rhode Island. I suspect that House is beating off recruiters eager to woo her away from Memphis now that the American Association of School Administrators has recognized her as 1999's Superintendent of the Year.

The long and short of it is that the waiver mentality will never get us anywhere. Obviously children need to be protected form educational charlatans. Yet the waiver mentality defines reform and change as deviations from the norm. It is the norm that is the problem.

Bringing Reform to Scale

The goal of school reform must be to establish the conditions under which such schools are the rule, not the exception. That is a daunting challenge. It will not be met by any of the existing reform formulas standing alone. Most of them accept the existing system largely as it is and try to fix it by adding on new components. Yet, as I learned with the Xerox 4000, that approach will not work.

What is needed is something much more significant, something that will break the school mold and really bring reform to scale. No one should underestimate just how hard this will be. Working within the framework of the common standards and expectations for student performance called for in chapter 10, we need simultaneously to redefine the term *public school* and to insist on innovation as a way of life in schools, offering families many more learning options. A way has to be found to replace timidity, bureaucracy, and going by the book with boldness, imagination, and vision. Finally, a fundamental principle of democracy must be instilled in education by letting parents choose the schools they think best for their children.

How do we as a society do that? I think we need to get serious about two bold strategies. First, we must encourage every school district in the country to make the school-design approach exemplified by New American Schools the normal approach to supporting innovation in the elementary school years. Whole-school designs at the elementary level should be normal education practice. As I noted in chapter 2, American students through grade four measure up well on international achievement assessments, something that might be expected given that public school administration was designed to manage the "common" elementary school. I judge that educators have become reasonably good at that.

It is in the elementary years, too, that whole-school designs appear to work best. Those of us who helped give birth to NAS and guided it into early adulthood are proud of what we have created. But like all parents, we have to make sure our children do not misjudge what they are capable of doing as they flex their wings. Diana Lam and the other superintendents active with New American Schools have been very candid about where NAS has succeeded and where it has found difficulty. As Lam acknowledged to the NAS board, reforming secondary schools is a much more difficult challenge than transforming an elementary school.

Several of the most successful NAS designs, such as Success for All/Roots and Wings, are oriented toward the elementary years. Even designs such as America's Choice and ATLAS Communities, which are intended to cover the gamut from kindergarten through grade twelve, rely on creating a solid foundation in the elementary grades. In a nutshell, the design-based approach shows great promise in the early years, whether the designs are from NAS or from the other whole-school models described in chapter 8.

But it would be wrong to say that these approaches show the same high promise at the secondary level. Some of the designs might have the right stuff; some might not. Here we need to be even bolder. I propose that at the secondary level we should acknowledge that any nonprofit group willing to be accountable for educating our children is performing a public service and is, in fact, a "public school."

A New Kind of Public School

By public secondary school, I mean any school chartered or contracted for by a state or local school district, supported with public funds, operated with public moneys, and accountable to public officials.

Today, a public school is an entity owned, financed, staffed, and operated by a unit of government. In the future, we should think of secondary public schools as any nonprofit entity chartered or contracted for by the state or district in the public's name. Such an entity is capable of operating in the public interest free of the red tape now strangling public education. It should be paid for by the public, accountable to the public, with its charter or contract routinely revoked when it stops serving public purposes or fails to meet its performance goals.

Creating Renewable, Innovative Schools

My proposal is similar to one developed recently by Paul Hill and his colleagues James Guthrie (Vanderbilt) and Larry Pierce (University of Washington).[2] Their essential argument is that the country has gone about as far as it can go in perfecting a bad system. Even if that system is polished to its maximum efficiency, it cannot do what is required of it in the modern world.

What I want is a system of secondary schools operating under renewable contracts for a specified period of time, not less than five years, and not more than ten. Because the portfolio of schools available to local citizens can be redesigned, reinvented, and reshaped almost continuously, local school systems should be encouraged to operate many different kinds of innovative schools.

Some contract schools could be very conventional, many of them directed and managed by the very teachers and administrators now frustrated by the current system. Other contract schools could be focused on specific curriculum areas, such as health careers, public safety, or environmental issues. Some might focus on traditional academic preparation, perhaps by emphasizing modern languages, classical languages, historical studies, or the great books. Others could offer nontraditional and original courses of study, emphasizing, for example, multicultural education, bilingual approaches, internships, experiential learning, expeditionary community programs, or single-sex or minority-oriented schooling.

My point is that there is real, even if sometimes modest, demand for each of these alternatives, particularly at the secondary level. But the current governance arrangements make it hard to meet that demand unless such programs are available virtually on demand at each school.

In considering a particular contract, the school board need not ask whether a school concept (such as environmental education, single-sex programs, multicultural education, or the great books) is the right concept for all students, or even for most students. It need not worry about whether some members of the community might dislike that particular school or even find its teachings distasteful. All the board needs to ask is whether a demand exists for the school; the people proposing the school have plausible credentials encouraging a belief that they can run it; and an evaluation and accountability system is in place that will permit the board to decide whether to renew the contract after the specified period or to terminate it and reopen the school under new management.

Public Accountability

It is of critical importance in this system that public officials retain the ultimate responsibility for school quality. These schools will be spending public money. They should be publicly accountable. Superintendents and school boards should be required to force substantial quality improvements or replace contractors who fail to deliver. When contracts come up for renewal, providers whose schools fall below some set level of performance should be eliminated from consideration for renewal. Contracting allows schools boards to do something they cannot now do: focus unrelentingly on the quality of instruction and learning in the lowest-performing schools.

I want also to repeat what I noted earlier about the obligation of states to carry out their responsibilities for equitable financing; protection of civil rights, health and safety of children; and the development of common standards for graduation, performance, and assessment. These requirements, naturally, would apply to contract schools, just as they do to today's independent schools.

Against a backdrop of common standards and assessments for all schools and students, contracts would need to be clear about several issues:

— Each contract should clearly delineate the goals the school seeks and the methods it will pursue to achieve those goals.

— In return for a contract providing the school with an amount equal to the per-pupil expenditures in that district (including instructional and capital costs), each contractor should specify the performance goals it expects to meet and the timetable on which they will be met.

— It should be understood that teachers work for the school, not the district, underlining teachers' new status as true professionals, who are independent, not career public employees.

— To avoid charges of discrimination, all school contracts should require random selection from the list of all student applicants. No school should be allowed to practice favoritism or to handpick only the ablest students.

— Schools should be required to help students experiencing academic difficulty and must continue helping students as long as they make the effort deemed essential by the school.

— To contain the tuition creep so evident in higher education, all contractors, including independent schools, would have to accept the per-pupil amount provided by the state as payment in full for students' educational costs.[3]

Changing Roles and Responsibilities

Contracting immediately changes the roles and functions of everyone involved. It completely alters the dynamics of school administration. Contracting requires public officials to make educational decisions on a school-by-school basis, rather than on the basis of policies that constrain all schools. It also requires public officials to do something they are not now required to do: periodically assess and do something about the quality of education offered in individual schools.

The very need to reexamine the contracts periodically alters the board's job fundamentally and changes the presuppositions of public officials about public schools. To date, the assumption is that because a school exists, it generally will continue to exist unless its enrollment base collapses. Contracting means that each school would have to justify its existence periodically by defending its educational performance.

The incentives for school board members shift from micromanaging individual schools and ensuring that the buses run on time to overseeing a management system oriented around school performance. School superintendents come to see their responsibility as encompassing all of the children in the community, including students enrolled in independent schools, not just children in "our" schools, that is, the ones the school district owns, manages, and staffs. State legislatures will be asked to redefine the role of school boards so that boards function as the overseers and managers of systems of "independent public schools."

The new system offers many possibilities for improving school performance while altering the dynamics of personnel allocation within systems. Too many school systems today are full of administrative bloat, with few, if any, incentives to encourage teachers to remain in the classroom instead of moving into central administration. Contracting encourages school officials to maximize the amount of money spent at the school building and to minimize the amount spent on central administration.

Smaller Schools, on a More Humane Scale

How large should these schools be? Schools in other countries offer some ideas. Dedication to the welfare of children—or to the ideal of education as a public trust—is not restricted to the United States. In Denmark, for example, where large proportions of students attend schools operated by nongovernmental organizations, a school enrolling as few as sixty students is entitled to receive state support.[4] That strikes me as a reasonable approach for thinking about appropriate levels of modest but real demand.

Given the one-size-fits-all aspect of the American school system, large, impersonal schools made administrative sense, even if the educational benefits were hard to find. Whether such schools genuinely provided economies of scale was beside the point; since every child was offered essentially the same process, why not provide it in the same building? But a system of schools dedicated to meeting as many diverse needs as possible almost demands that school boards encourage the establishment of much smaller and more humane environments.

The Role of Choice

Above all, installing whole-school designs at the elementary level and contracting for secondary schools totally shifts the balance of power within public education. Such changes fundamentally alter the role of the parent. Here choice enters the picture. Offering different options does not mean much unless families can choose among them. Because many different kinds of educational options would be available, parents should be able to take advantage of the opportunity to choose among credible alternatives.

Care must be used in defining the term *choice*. It means different things to different people. Some people believe that choice has been fully defined with charter or magnet school options. Others believe choice means vouchers. And some believe choice involves subsidies to permit students to attend private schools. Quite a few use the word "choice" to mean access to for-profit educational entities.

Choice in the context of whole-school designs or contract schools is not any of these things. By choice, I do not simply mean charter schools or magnet schools as they are currently understood—a very limited concept, which defines school innovation as a deviation. The contract ideal described here would make every school a charter school. I do not mean *vouchers* either, as that term is currently used—a few thousand dollars in tax breaks to subsidize middle- and upper-middle-income families already spending up to $10,000 or more at private schools. Nor do I mean using public money to subsidize partial payments for students attending private schools or to extend access to for-profit educational efforts.

What I am proposing is not a system of vouchers because the funds are intended to cover the full costs of education. Vouchers (such as Pell Grants in higher education or tax breaks of various kinds that have been proposed for elementary and secondary education) normally only subsidize part of the cost. Nor is this proposal likely to turn into a subsidy for the well-to-do, because it requires independent contractors and schools to accept the per-pupil payment as payment in full.

Finally, the proposal does not incorporate for-profit entities because I have seen no convincing evidence that the private sector has been able to do a better job than those in public schools for the same amount of money. I think we have to be sensitive to community concerns here, too. Many members of the public are understandably uncomfortable with the idea of applying the profit motive to children.

In a nutshell, choice to me means that parents should have the freedom to select their children's schooling from a variety of new kinds of public schools at both the elementary and secondary levels. Such schools would have to agree to accept state per-pupil funding as full payment for students' educational costs.

Religious Schools

The decision to include all eligible nonprofit groups obviously includes religious schools of all kinds, from long-established Catholic, Lutheran, and Jewish schools to relatively new schools established by fundamentalist Christians.[5] I have wrestled with this issue for a decade. As a matter of conscience, I believe religious schools must be included. As a practical matter, they should be left out, because including them creates all kinds of political problems. In the end, conscience wins.

It is time we were honest about this. In the name of separation of church and state, society has created a schooling system that is hostile to religious values. Despite the personal beliefs of individual teachers and administrators, the system is not simply neutral about matters of faith and the moral dimensions of learning; it is actively opposed to them. And in the name of public education, our school system, society, and courts have displayed a fairly consistent and long-standing prejudice against Catholics that can only be termed shameful.[6] Practically every reputable historian of American education acknowledges the anti-Catholic bias built into public education since the nineteenth century.

I don't know where the current court debates about religion in the schools will end up. Jurisprudence in this area is such an incomprehensible mess it invites public ridicule.[7] Public funds may be spent in church-affiliated day-care centers but not on kindergarten classes. Federal aid is available to help students attend private and church-affiliated colleges and universities, but not to attend independent schools. Federal Title I funds for compensatory education can be used to help children attending religious schools, but often state funds cannot. Federal Title I funds can be used to purchase textbooks, materials, and equipment for low-income students in parochial schools, but federal courts have upheld recent challenges to including parochial schools in a new federal program to wire schools to the Internet. In some areas, state and local funds can be used to provide transportation and textbooks to children in parochial schools, but elsewhere these practices violate state law. Perhaps the ultimate irony in this whole area was a decision by the U.S. Supreme Court upholding a decision that approved the use of public funds for textbooks, but decided that maps were out of the question. Senator Daniel Patrick Moynihan of New York was left wondering: "What about atlases?"

In the face of this confusion, what is one to make of the June 1998 Wisconsin Supreme Court decision permitting up to 15,000 Milwaukee students to attend private schools (including religious schools) at taxpayer expense?[8] By a 4-2 ruling, the justices held that Milwaukee's program did not promote religion or link church and state. They held that a student qualified for the program because he or she was poor and enrolled in Milwaukee Public Schools, "not because he or she was a Catholic, a Jew, a Muslim, or an atheist." The following November, the U.S. Supreme Court, by an 8-1 vote, refused to second-guess the decision, letting it stand.

A layman like myself cannot know where the Supreme Court will ultimately land on these issues, but its acceptance of the Milwaukee situation appears to be a significant straw in the wind. I do know, however, that in matters educational, the U.S. Supreme Court has been monumentally (and disastrously) wrong in the past and has later corrected itself. The court's historic 1954 *Brown* v. *Topeka Board of Education* decision was a direct repudiation of the misguided support for "separate but equal" schools it offered in *Plessy* v. *Ferguson* in 1896. The Court's decision in the Milwaukee case may be an isolated decision. Nonetheless, I believe the court's past positions on school aid and separation of church and state have been as misguided as its earlier decisions on "separate but equal," and I hold out hope that its decision in the Milwaukee case foreshadows a different approach in the future.

I stood for choice in 1988 in *Winning the Brain Race*, and that is where I stand today. Why? I am for choice because states compel school attendance. Because the states require parents to send their children to school, and because the states provide, on average, 50 percent or more of school funding, state law should provide parents (and teachers, too, for that matter) with choices in the kind of public schools their children attend.

The choice that is good enough for children of the well-to-do and the affluent should also be available to the children of the poor and the disenfranchised. Until somebody can explain to me why the children of national politicians (of both parties) can attend independent schools without threatening the national interest but the children of the rest of us cannot, I will continue to stand up for choice.

There is another reason, too. Choice will encourage competition among the public schools. Many people are horrified by that idea, but I am not. Competition is the whole point. The truth is that until the Japanese started driving Xerox, Motorola, and Detroit's Big Three to the wall, each of these companies acted pretty dumb and happy. Public schools have been acting that way, too. The loss of patronage and income is a necessary first step toward improving any low-performing institution, whether it produces goods such as copiers, televisions, or automobiles or provides a service such as educating the public's children.

Choice poses one potential problem that needs attention. Al Shanker used to bring it up quite a lot, and I believe it is a legitimate concern. He used to worry about hate groups of various kinds, neo-Nazis or skinheads, getting their hands on public funds to operate a school. Others worry that exotic religions, fundamentalist followers of Islam for example, might seek a charter.

Let's separate these two issues. I do not support discrimination against members of the Catholic or Jewish faiths, and I will not support discrimination against fundamentalist Muslims or Christians either. That is all there is to say about that. Religious discrimination cannot be tolerated, no matter how "odd" some people might think the beliefs of others are.

Hate groups present quite a different issue. Here I rely on the definition of an eligible nonprofit. Under Internal Revenue Service regulations, eligible nonprofit groups are those organized and operated exclusively for charitable, religious, educational, scientific, or literary purposes. Groups that advance public safety, foster national or international sports competitions, or work to prevent cruelty to children or animals are also considered to be eligible nonprofits under the IRS regulations.

The IRS does not normally hand out nonprofit eligibility to hate groups. It lists several examples of qualifying groups: nonprofit old-age homes, parent-teacher associations, charitable hospitals, alumni associations, schools, chapters of the Red Cross or Salvation Army, boys' and girls' clubs, and churches. Clearly, by the IRS standards, neo-Nazis and skinheads need not apply. Suppose, however, that a hate group slipped through the net, seeking nonprofit status, for example, under the guise of an educational or charitable purpose. How would this new system of governance handle this problem?

Rather than creating this problem, I think contracting simply makes the problem transparent. Individual principals and teachers go off the reservation now, teaching white kids that black kids are inferior, teaching black kids that white politicians do not represent their interests, or banning interracial dates at proms. Under contracting, such acts are clear violations of the contract, and public officials have the authority to cancel the offending school's contract forthwith. Armed with that power, it is unlikely that vigilant public officials would have to threaten more than once.

The American education paradox is that public schools, celebrated as a bulwark of democracy, do not embody the democratic principle of choice in their operation. Shanker may have said it best in 1989.[9] The head of the American Federation of Teachers was not talking about private school choice or aid to help students attend religious schools, both of which he opposed, but he got the general idea right.

We ought to retain only the school regulations governing health, safety, and civil rights, Shanker suggested, and encourage practically unrestricted choice for teachers and students. Why? There were a lot of reasons, he said, beginning with the political reality that the public and its officials were getting fed up with the poor education performance of the nation's public school students. If educators did not make these changes on their own, he warned, they would be forced to accept them. But in a larger sense, Shanker also appealed to the better angels of our nature. Why choice? "Because it's a basic American value," he said.

Benefits of Choice

Will choice work? Only time will tell. But it seems to work reasonably well everywhere else it has been tried. In Australia, Belgium, Canada, France, Germany, Great Britain, Ireland, and the Netherlands, much greater flexibility and choice among publicly funded schools has been the norm for decades. Catholics in Canada, for example, operate a publicly funded school system that is considered to be a "system of public schools for Catholics." My proposal includes religious schools, in part because the Canadian example demonstrates just how narrow Americans' common vision of what it means to be "public" has become.

An examination of school choice in six nations, conducted for the U.S. Department of Education, concluded that parents everywhere want to be able to choose the schools their children attend, that publicly supported choice is often a matter of fairness (since the well-to-do already enjoy it), and that minority parents have the greatest stake in publicly funded educational alternatives.[10] I was particularly struck by two of the conclusions of this study. It noted, first, that in several different societies, the availability of parental choice has a positive effect upon the quality of schooling available. That confirms what most of us who support greater school choice have assumed. In the market of educational ideas, competition is a good thing. Everyone accepts competition as a good thing in higher education. Why would it not also be a good thing in public schools?

Second, the study concluded that choice increases societal support for schools by reducing the level of conflict over the purposes and control of schools.[11] This finding is truly noteworthy. In the furor of the fierce partisan and ideological debates about the role and purposes of public schools in the United States, opponents of choice have argued that it will ring the death-knell for public education as we know it. They have it exactly backwards. According to this study, choice is a sort of safety valve, on both the political left and right, for people who feel so strongly about education that they are willing to wage ideological war over its basic premises. By minimizing conflict over the nature of education offered at individual schools, choice, paradoxically, increases societal support for public schools generally.

Choice works in the United States, as well. A handful of school districts in the United States that have committed themselves to choice have made it work. In Moses Lake, Washington, for example, choice among schools helped create a new social compact between the schools and the community, according to the late Ben Edlund, who served as superintendent for many years. "All thirteen schools in Moses Lake are essentially 'charter' or 'contract' schools," Edlund reported at Paul Hill's Lake Union meeting. "We began in 1987, before the terms were invented, and we invited the community into the discussion. We spoke of a new 'social contract' between the public and the schools. Then we turned 97 percent of the district's funds over to the schools. One school doesn't have a principal; another did away with grouping students automatically by grade; a third got into project learning. The long and short of it is that we got efficiency, effectiveness, innovation, and vastly improved school performance."

In Massachusetts, Wisconsin, and New York City, choice has been demonstrated to work as well. A research team from the John F. Kennedy School of Government at Harvard and the Institute for Public Policy at George Mason University in Virginia recently examined the interdistrict choice program put into practice in Massachusetts in 1991; it is now the largest program of its kind in the United States.[12] The researchers looked into the effects of competition on program improvements in the school districts; why parents and students left one district for another; the effects of choice on racial balance; and whether students from all backgrounds take advantage of their new-found ability to choose. The answers to these questions were so promising that the authors recommended expanding the program to permit all school districts in the state to participate and improving advertising so that more parents, particularly in low-income areas, might be made aware of their options.

An equally encouraging story is recounted by researchers examining privately supported private school choice in Milwaukee. In addition to the Milwaukee Parental Choice Program backed by Howard Fuller, an organization known as PAVE (Partners to Advance Values in Education) provides scholarship assistance to low-income families equivalent to half-tuition to any elementary or secondary private or parochial school in Milwaukee.

The program was launched in the 1992–93 academic year; research over the first five years of the program reveals several extremely promising findings.

— Program participation has grown from a total of 2,089 grants in the first year (made on a first-come, first-served basis) to more than 4,400.

— Parental involvement is remarkable: more than 90 percent of parents reported involvement with the schools in a variety of ways; more than 90 percent also reported reading to their children and working on mathematics problems with them.

— More than 90 percent of parents are satisfied with the schools their children attend.

— Students are doing well academically, as measured by standardized tests and teacher, parent, and student perceptions. In fact, PAVE students scored higher than did samples of Milwaukee Parental Choice Program students, low-income Milwaukee Public Schools (MPS) students, and all MPS students.

— About half the parents had children enrolled in both public and private schools, a modest indication that parents choose the option they think best suited to the needs of each of their children.

But perhaps the most encouraging evidence is to be found in Harlem, New York. When educators look for success in New York City schools, the first district normally cited is the famous District 4. People are inevitably impressed with the way that district's alternative schools changed the lives of children growing up in one of the country's most challenging neighborhoods.[13] My friend Deborah Meier was a big part of this success, but she was only one of dozens of District 4 educators who started creating a series of small, tightly knit schools in the 1970s. Each of these schools had a focused curriculum and engaged parents and the community. The district, under the leadership of deputy superintendent Seymour ("Sy") Fliegel, encouraged families to choose the schools their children would attend.

By 1984 the district had twenty-nine alternative schools. District 4 went from being dead last among New York City School districts (thirty-second out of thirty-two districts) to fifteenth in student achievement. Reading scores soared, violence and absenteeism plummeted, and District 4's students began to be accepted in record numbers in college. What happened in Harlem can happen anywhere if we can find the will to persevere.

Above all, contracting responds to Howard Fuller's dilemma. His essential complaint was that despite the notorious underperformance of many schools, nobody did anything about it. As Al Shanker used to say, public education was the only large enterprise he knew of where if you did well, nothing happened; and if you did poorly, nothing happened, either. A system of performance-based contracts requires public officials to make something happen.

CHAPTER TWELVE

AGENDA FOR CHANGE, PART III:

Ten Ground Rules to Advance Education Reform

THE DIFFICULTIES INVOLVED when real change is let out of the box should not obscure the truth: Despite differences of opinion within the education and policy communities, a strikingly broad consensus on the shape of school reform exists. In my two decades of involvement with school improvement—starting as a corporate CEO, deepening as a subcabinet official, and continuing to this day as chairman of New American Schools—I have watched this consensus take shape and broaden.

There is consensus on the national education goals. Some of us are still inclined to want to tweak them here and there. But presidents from both parties, governors from all fifty states, both houses of Congress, and many of the nation's business leaders have all endorsed them. They are acceptable as they are and should be left alone.

I think there is also broad agreement that many things are just more difficult today than they were in the past. It is harder to be a kid; it is harder to be a parent; and, because both of those things are harder, it is harder to be a teacher, too.

Finally, I think there is a reasonable consensus about what works. The country has nearly fifty years of educational research and analysis of effective ways of educating American students. It is time to put that investment to work. What is lacking is a way to deliver it widely. This book's recommendations to harness systemic reform to innovation and choice are intended to fill that gap.

But my experience tells me that these broad areas of consensus need to be pushed farther. I think the time has come for those of us who have been arguing for radical change in American schools to admit that we have done a disservice by talking about "schools" as if they were all the same. We need to respect a few distinctions.

One reason too many people may be willing to believe "the nation is at risk, but my school is fine" is that we have confused them. Analysts and critics report that the quality of the nation's schools has put the country's children at risk and then support their argument with data on the performance of secondary school students. Parents look at their children in second grade and wonder what the critics are talking about. In fact, recent international comparisons, including the TIMSS results, indicate that American elementary schools stand up well and perhaps are superior. A casual observer would never know that from the reform discussion, in which the critics condemn (and the defenders uphold) all levels of schooling.

It is time to be up front about this: Elementary schooling in America can undoubtedly be improved, but the nation's educational problem is most acute in the middle and secondary schools. Ask any parent and they'll tell you the same thing: Little kids are demanding but pretty easy to deal with—and a lot of fun, to boot. Teenagers, in contrast, have been called "hormones in sneakers." Children's entry into adolescence sends many of their mothers and fathers into the nightmare years of parenthood. The teenage years are the nightmare years of our national educational dilemma, too.

It is also time to acknowledge that Washington is not the solution. When I left Xerox to join the Bush administration, I was convinced government could accomplish a lot more than it was ever really designed to do. Frankly, I didn't understand the politics of schools or the dynamics of school governance. Because I had succeeded at Xerox, I thought the skills I had used in the private setting were portable to a public one. But I was to receive a lesson in the complexity of changing ingrained ways of doing things in the schools.

Don't misunderstand me. The bully pulpit of the national government can do a lot. It can keep the issue of education alive in the public's mind. Government must make sure that civil rights are respected. The Department of Education can try to ensure that vulnerable children, the poor and those with disabilities, receive the attention they need. It is the only government entity that can support national research, collect national data, and make agreements with international bodies such as TIMSS to participate in international studies. But beyond that, the federal government is fairly limited. Washington is neither the source of the problems in the nation's schools nor the solution. The public education system cannot be reformed at the national level. Change will come about state by state, school system by school system, school by school, and even classroom by classroom.

That is why you and the other people reading this book are so important. The schools will never change to suit the needs of our children without your support, and the support of people just like you. Everyone needs to be involved—not just parents, but also grandparents, aunts and uncles, people without children, and academic leaders and government officials, too.

What You Can Do

There is a standard laundry list for parental involvement in schools that most respected education authorities endorse. In the main, the laundry list takes the status quo for granted and advocates a set of unexceptional activities that should, in fact, be standard practice for all citizens and all parents. This list includes such old chestnuts as taking the trouble to vote in school board elections or running for office yourself; making appointments with the local school superintendent to let him or her know of your concerns; volunteering as a classroom aid or individual tutor; and becoming active in parents' coalitions and textbook and curriculum review committees.

Each of these recommendations is good advice. It is very distressing, for example, to learn that voter participation in school board elections is dreadful. Many school board members are elected with the votes of fewer than 10 percent of the eligible electorate. But even if each of these recommendations were acted on earnestly by every citizen in the United States, little would change. The system would run a little more smoothly, but the schools still would not be consciously striving for world-class standards or performance.

Following is a road map for citizen involvement in schools. It consists of ten commonsense ground rules you and your family can use to advance the education reform agenda outlined in this book. It is followed by some direct advice for business and community leaders and public officials.

The ground rules are organized into two main sections. The first five ground rules are directed at parents; the second five are aimed at the general public, including those who are not parents. Here, we ask you to help parents insist that the schools do their part.

Do Your Part

Parents are a child's first teachers. The environment for learning they create is every bit as important as the school environment.

1. Do No Harm

The most important admonition Hippocrates made to physicians was, "First, do no harm." Most parents already heed that advice. Every parent wants to do the right thing, and most do. But some parents are so deeply troubled they have difficulty helping their children. Sadly, many parents, not always young single mothers, do not know how to respond to their children's needs. Tragically, sometimes parents hurt their own children.

A fairly common problem, particularly with young single parents, revolves around adults who literally do not know how to raise a child. Often the parents, single or married, are little more than children themselves. There was a time when the extended family, made up of grandparents, brothers and sisters, and aunts and uncles could literally demonstrate to new parents how to do it. They modeled how to hold the baby; how to change the diaper, and how to encourage good behavior instead of walloping children every time they stepped out of line. But in most cases, the extended family no longer exists. If parents are unsure about how to proceed, they need to seek guidance from doctors, social service agencies, even local libraries.

A much more difficult issue is child abuse. Most of us would like to pretend such abuse does not exist. Unfortunately, it does. Abusive parents can be found in every community in the country. It is not clear whether the startling rise in reported cases of child abuse and neglect in the United States is something new or the result of more rigorous reporting requirements. What is undeniable is that a shocking number of children, many of them infants and toddlers, are subject to appalling abuse in their own homes. Each year a handful make headlines because parents or guardians, or friends or neighbors, beat or torture them to death. Sometimes the abuse is physical, sometimes it is sexual. Often, it is emotional abandonment of the child.

I find it hard to understand how children subjected to such treatment can be expected to learn at all. Some of them do, of course. It is a tribute to human resiliency that some of those who survive these brutalities emerge from them relatively intact. But these problems are not educational problems, although the school often brings them to the attention of local authorities. Guardians, relatives, friends, and neighbors have to take the lead in protecting these children. If parents are so out of control that they are a threat to their own children, others must intervene.

2. Send Your Child to School Ready to Learn

When Roland Chevalier, whom we met in chapter 10, reports that he sees six-year-old children who have never been to a doctor, he describes a reality with which practically every teacher and administrator in the United States is familiar—the reality of a child arriving at school without the basic foundation for success. Chevalier is talking about lack of even minimally adequate health care for children. But the readiness problem extends far beyond well-baby care and inoculations. At its most basic level, readiness revolves around ensuring that the cognitive foundation for the child's learning has been laid. Early childhood experiences are the key to building future success.

In recent years neuroscientists have made substantial progress in understanding how the human brain develops.[1] They have found that babies are born with all the brain cells they will ever have, that they begin shedding those cells as the brain begins to wire itself, and that the child's basic neural wiring is complete at the age of five. That explains why infants and children are such remarkable sponges in their ability to absorb and make sense of new information. Before children ever arrive at kindergarten, practically all of them have mastered language, one of the most intellectually challenging tasks they will undertake in their lives.

Dr. Katherine Bick, an internationally known neurobiologist and consultant to the Charles A. Dana Foundation, thinks of brain development as akin to building Heath Kits, the old mail-order radio sets that buyers used to put together themselves.[2] "You follow these vague directions and don't know if it'll work till you turn it on," Bick told a meeting of state legislators in 1997. When a child's brain is turned on in school, it should work, she says.

There is no secret to how parents can help turn on their child's brain. The process begins with parents' love, something no school can provide. It continues with the things that most parents do without conscious thought as their children grow: babbling and baby-talk to introduce the infant to sound; displays of vivid colors and black and white contrasts to help the baby's eyes develop; reading to children every day so that they are introduced to narrative and to shapes, textures, colors, and even music and sounds in today's children's books; getting the child ready for reading by teaching them their colors, numbers, and letters; and introducing the child to the joys of motion through play, music, and dance.

The most important thing parents can do to advance school reform is to send their own children to school ready to learn. Start by making sure they are ready for learning at the age of five.

Then make sure they are ready to learn every day they leave the house for school. Readiness to learn is not just for five-year-olds. What about your child in middle school or high school? Are television hours limited? Have you checked on homework assignments? Have you maintained contact with your child's teachers so that if problems develop, you will be on top of them? Have you asked for a summer reading list to make sure your child does not fall out of the habit? School readiness is a 365-day-a-year habit throughout your child's school years.

3. Ask the Right Questions

Most parents, men and women, are intimidated when the blank, bureaucratic gaze of the school is turned on them. Parents are dealing from a position of weakness. They think the school personnel are the experts. Subconsciously, parents are right back in front of their first-grade teacher, who knows that they have been misbehaving. Because the school knows their children, it knows something about them as parents. Maybe the experts are finally going to reveal how inadequate they are in that role. Or perhaps they are going to reveal a child's behavioral or other problems to which the parents were oblivious.

But all of this is just our anxiety getting out of control. We need to have much more confidence in ourselves. Nobody knows or understands our children as well as we do. When it comes to our kids, we are the experts.

Many of us are so intimidated by the schools, that we don't know how to make them respond to us. A good start can be made by asking the right questions. Here are ten questions you have a perfect right to ask at your school:

— What skills and knowledge will my child be expected to master this year in key subjects such as math, science, history, and English?

— How will I know if my child is making good progress?

— How will you report to me on how well my child is doing?

— What kinds of tests do you give, when are they given, what do they reveal, and how are they used?

— How does this school connect its curriculum and classroom work to demanding academic standards from national bodies?

— Besides learning from books, what practical skills will my child learn that can be used at home, in the community, or at work? How will my child be prepared for further learning after high school?

— Tell me how teaching and learning has changed in this school in response to computers and new telecommunications technologies?

— How are student differences accommodated? What do you do to help students with disabilities or with different learning styles, backgrounds, and languages?

— How are parents involved in making decisions at this school?

— What are this school's discipline policies? If my child gets into trouble, what happens?

Not only do you as a parent have a perfect right to ask these questions, you have a perfect right to expect them to be taken seriously. I would worry about any school that balked at the questions. And I would worry just as much about a school that implied the answers were too complex for you to understand, too difficult to obtain, or simply none of your business. If I received any of those answers, I would be on the telephone to the superintendent and school board immediately.

4. Understand What Is Available

As a parent, you cannot be an expert on every innovation coming down the educational pike. In fact, educators themselves, particularly teachers, have become so worn down by succeeding waves of education reform that many of the latest innovations have probably passed them by too.

But it is not unreasonable to expect you to have general knowledge of the broad shape and outline of the reform movement. Appendix B clarifies the terms of the debate by providing a brief tour of the complex standards and assessment horizon. Appendix C defines some of the principal written and organizational resources for school reform. It lists key reading resources and the main reform actors, describing what they are up to and providing addresses so that you can obtain additional information. Among the resources available to you are:

—Detailed curriculum content standards from key professional groups in key subjects such as English, mathematics, science, the arts, and geography.

—Annual reports from the National Goals Panel defining the nation's educational goals and outlining progress toward attaining them. (The National Goals Panel was created by federal statute in 1994 to track the progress the nation is making in achieving the national education goals.)

—Explicit models of new break-the-mold schools, and assistance with implementing them, from diverse organizations ranging from New American Schools to the Coalition for Essential Schools.

—Sophisticated, off-the-shelf testing and assessment systems tied to new standards.

—Thoughtful and reflective commentaries on the practical challenges of implementing schoolwide reform and how to meet them.

So do not be intimidated if school personnel shrug their shoulders when you ask if the English or mathematics curriculum reflects the latest thinking. Believe it or not, they might not know where the latest thinking can be found. But you do. If need be, tear out the appendixes and provide them to school personnel as a contribution to the school's curriculum research. For your child's sake, you cannot accept "I don't know" as an answer.

5. Demand Choices

Finally you must understand that you will never be provided with choices unless you demand them. It is okay here to pound the table. Here you must shift your attention from your relationship with your children and their individual schools to the school system of which they are a part and the political structure that oversees them. Your local principal probably cannot do anything about choice; but your school board and state legislature almost certainly can.

You must demand choice. And you must make it clear that you mean choice among new kinds of public schools.

Choice, as Al Shanker observed, is a basic American value. We Americans respect it in representative government. It is the cornerstone of our free market economy. We insist on it in the cars we drive, the television shows we watch, and the religious services we attend. We even take it for granted in higher education, which we regularly hail as the envy of the world. Choice is as American as apple pie, a fundamental principle of our way of life that should be reflected in our public schools.

The internationally respected public opinion pollster Daniel Yankelovich warns that the public no longer feels the schools are public in the sense of being "owned" by the American people. "People feel schools are controlled by the unions and the professionals in them," he says. "In some significant way, public schools are not the public's schools anymore."[3]

If this perception is to change, you must say that you want control of the schools back. You will be speaking for most Americans. Recent polls indicate that most people think parents should have the right to choose the local schools their children attend. By "local schools," most people, I think, mean public schools. Even more surprising, the annual poll conducted by the education honorary society Phi Delta Kappa shows that the proportion of the public that favors allowing parents to send their child to a private school at public expense nearly doubled between 1993 and 1997. Support grew from 24 to 44 percent while opposition dropped, just as steadily from 74 to 50 percent.[4]

In fact, choice seems to be even more popular among parents than among the general public, and more popular still among minority parents. Indeed, the closer one gets to minority parents in urban areas, the more urgent is their sense of rage and desperation about the state of the schools their children are forced to attend.

So do not accept the argument that choice is somehow the enemy of public education. It might save public education from itself. And do not buy the argument that choice benefits only the affluent. Low-income minority parents need choice too. Above all, do not accept the line of thinking that says, "This is the way we've always done it."

Just keep repeating the following to yourself and your elected officials until all of you get tired of it: If we keep on doing what we've always done, we'll keep on getting what we've always had.

Insist that Schools Do Their Part

Regardless of how well parents do their part, at some point they need the help of the larger society to make sure the schools do theirs.

6. Provide an Adult for Every Child

David Hawkins is a sociologist at the University of Washington. Early in his career as a probation officer dealing with fifteen-year-old students, he said, "I felt I was running an ambulance service at the bottom of a cliff. I would patch up a handful of kids and the judge would send more over." Hawkins began thinking about medical models and about how much cheaper and easier it is to prevent cardiovascular disease than it is to pay for by-pass surgery. "Over the long haul in the last twenty-five years," he says, "there's been a major change in people's life-styles and a 40 percent reduction in cardiovascular disease." Hawkins stresses that we know what helps kids in communities and schools. The essential thing, he says, appears to be convincing young people that adults care about them. Every child needs an adult advocate, he concludes.[5]

Deborah Meier reached the same conclusion years ago. Meier was for many years one of the outstanding school principals in New York, indeed in the United States. She is still an outstanding principal, but now she is in Boston, where she was helping create a flexible new elementary school, part of a joint school district–union effort called the Pilot School project, when I talked to her in 1998.[6] Several years ago, when she was still principal of New York's Central Park East Secondary School, she told me she believed individual schools had become too big for their own good. Schools should be smaller, she thought.

She picked up that theme again when we spoke in 1998. "In smaller schools," she said, "the principal could really know all the teachers, and the teachers could really know all the students." She suggested that all of us, the public and educators alike, should look askance at any school with more than about twenty teachers and 400 students. "If you can't get all the teachers around the same big table in one room and discuss every kid in the school," said Meier, "something's wrong."

Today, I am more convinced than ever that people like Hawkins and Meier are on the right track. Children need adult advocates. Every school, says Meier, needs to be organized so that adults can "know each student, their family, and their work well." Good schools succeed, she insists, "because they make sure each kid has several advocates, mentors, and a relationship with each of them." That is the great thing about sports and coaches, she notes. "Athletics surrounds kids with a group of adults who care about them." And, it needs to be said, most coaches also care about performance and do not want to hear excuses for poor performance.

At least one adult who cares about every child. Most children have more, and for most of them the most important adult is a parent, guardian, or other member of the family. But some children do not have anyone. How do your local schools stay in touch with the needs of individual students? Do not accept an answer that revolves largely around the guidance counselor. Most guidance counselors have far too many students assigned to them to know what is going on with any of them.

Find out how well your schools know their students as individuals. It might be the most important thing you do.

7. Stand Up for Standards and High Expectations

All of us must stand up for high educational standards and expectations for student performance. At the request of the business community in 1996, the nation's governors agreed to continue pushing for rigorous standards. But I doubt that either the agreement or ACHIEVE, the organization it spawned, will amount to much unless the public backs it up. All of us should get behind standards.

What should these standards look like? The following give a general idea. They are not very complicated.[7]

—By the end of third grade your child should be able to read.

—Your eighth grader should be comfortable with proportionality, basic algebra, and geometry.

—By ninth grade your child should be able to read stories in *USA Today* and discuss them knowledgeably with you.

—Your eleventh-grade daughter should be able to discuss the principles underlying the American Revolution and describe how the Declaration of Independence and the Federalist Papers were related to it.

—By senior year, at the latest, your son should be able to hold an intelligent conversation with someone in another language.

—Your child should score at least at the international level of eight-, thirteen-, and seventeen-year-olds on the tests used by the Third International Mathematics and Science Study.

Some students will find it easier than others to master demanding material. That is only to be expected. The schools we have inherited have tried to avoid this challenge. They have been content to let results vary while holding time and resources constant. Schools in the future should make high standards the constant, varying time and resources to meet the needs of individual students.[8]

Why do we need standards and high expectations? In too many ways, the secondary school diploma in America has become little more than a certificate of attendance. It is handed out not on the basis of proficiency, but to anyone who stays the course. It is the educational equivalent of a driver's license. Practically everyone gets one at a certain age. Then we expect our graduates to compete with graduates of other nations who have had to demonstrate competence and skill in key subjects.

The schools should also do away with tracking. Tracking, dividing children into learning groups by age and ability level, narrows educational experiences, constricts students' futures, and wastes human potential. Yet too wide a spread in achievement in a single classroom is not good; indeed, that is the greatest complaint of elementary school teachers. So I would encourage putting an end to tracking and age grouping generally, as well as undifferentiated heterogeneous grouping, in favor of grouping children by demonstrated achievement as soon as they show they are ready to master the material.

Gerry House understood the pernicious effects of tracking and put a stop to it Memphis. In a district that is 84 percent African American and mostly poor, she insisted that "all our kids be prepared for a high-tech world, for future work or further education. We insisted that everyone finish high school with at least three years of college preparatory mathematics and science. That means biology, chemistry, and physics. It means two years of algebra and a year of geometry. And it means something else as well: We didn't have time during the day for all those other math courses that were simply euphemisms for arithmetic. So you won't find Business Mathematics and Math for Life in Memphis schools."

All students are capable of learning and all of them are capable of mastering a broad liberal education that will fit them for anything they want to do in life. Educators should be embarrassed to have conspired with the public to create the achievement disaster we are trying to fix today.

A few simple concepts can light the road ahead. All students can learn. Content, not process, is what counts. Literature, the arts, history, mathematics, and science are essential to every student's intellectual and moral growth. And good teachers and good textbooks are the single most important element of the school. Don't let anyone try to tell you anything different.

8. Demand Accountability

I am genuinely very troubled by Holly Jones' account of how New York State set ridiculously low benchmarks for third-grade mathematics performance and then reassured the public that 95 percent of third-graders were doing just fine. What is one to make of this? Is this simply incompetence, or is it cynicism at work? In the private sector it would be labeled for what it is—educational fraud.

Much greater accountability is needed in American public education. Whenever a new reform idea involving greater consumer choice is discussed, opponents stop the conversation dead in its tracks by asking how these schools will be accountable to the public. Almost never is it mentioned that the existing system is rarely held accountable.

The best way to hold schools accountable for their performance is to institute a statewide testing program, with the results for individual schools and districts made public. Because it is institutional accountability (not detailed information on the performance of each student) that is being sought, I would be satisfied with a sampling framework that ensured that every school and every district participated every three years with a sample of its students from selected grades. To provide some basic reference points, the age of the children should parallel the age of the participants in the TIMSS and NAEP evaluations: nine-year-olds, thirteen-year-olds, and seventeen-year-olds.

The results of this statewide testing program should be published for each school and district, with enough information provided to tell parents and citizens what was tested and why it was important. The testing program should be keyed to state curriculum frameworks, and questions should be piloted extensively to make sure they are valid and reliable.

It is time to stop letting educators pull the wool over their own eyes. A little sunshine on how well our students are performing will work wonders to raise achievement.

9. Play Truth or Consequences: Insist on Assessment with Teeth

Similar considerations underlie the concern with student assessment. Here we are interested in detailed information about the performance of individual students. The assessment system, as opposed to the statewide accountability system, must be designed to give teachers, administrators, parents, and students themselves a very accurate picture of the student's strengths and weaknesses by subject. Of necessity, assessment information is private. It is for the student, his or her parents, and the school.

In putting such assessment systems in place, schools can draw on two resources. The first consists of "Instructional Learning Systems," high-tech assessment mechanisms that test students' knowledge and skills and loop back through areas of weakness to help correct them. The second consists of several new assessment systems pioneered in Vermont in the late 1980s and expanded and improved by groups such as the New Standards Project. These systems encourage "authentic assessment," often consisting of detailed portfolios of student work, actual writing samples and research projects, and the results of performances.[9]

If assessment systems are to succeed, they must have some teeth. Old habits often die hard. The practice of "social promotion" of students, passing them along whether or not they have mastered the material, must come to an end. Many educators believe that after first grade retaining students in grade is counterproductive. They may have a point. But moving students along without the necessary foundation for more advanced work is equally counterproductive.

The new assessments need to be backed up by insisting that students who need additional work put in the time. For them, a longer school day, work on Saturday mornings, or extensive review in summer school may be required. That does not sound like much fun. But properly approached with skilled teachers, it does not have to be drudgery. Besides, what is really not much fun is maturing into an unemployed adult while better-prepared people run rings around you.

10. Look for Fairness in Funding

Equity in funding is one of the most contentious issues in American public schooling. State constitutions may guarantee equal financing, and state courts may try to require it, but glaring inequities in expenditures per student continue to bedevil the schools.

Americans like to think of themselves as fair people, and they are. But when it comes to school finance, they have lost faith in themselves. It offends basic notions of fairness for some schools to have Olympic swimming pools while others are rat-infested and unsafe, open despite violations of health and fire codes. Within the same state, some districts spend four times as much per student as others, and some schools receive twice as much in per-student funding. We can and should do better.

The state share of public school funding has increased quite dramatically in the last generation. In 1970 the average state share was about 10 percent of school funding; today the average state share exceeds 50 percent. Much of this increase has been an effort to equalize expenditures among school districts, most of which rely on local property taxes to finance their schools. School funding is one of the most difficult and complicated issues in public finance. But in a nutshell, citizens in districts with high property values can often support their schools quite handsomely with relatively modest tax effort, while those in districts with low property value cannot spend as much, even if they tax themselves at much higher rates.

It is time to bite the bullet on this issue. Although school districts are local, they are units of state government. States cannot absolve themselves of responsibility for financing inequities. That is simply hiding behind legalisms. Moreover, the increase in the state proportion in the last twenty to thirty years indicates that states understand their obligation.

My proposal is to follow this logic where it leads. States should assume responsibility for full state funding of education, equalizing public expenditures across the state, and leaving local property tax revenues in local communities to be used as local citizens see fit. Following this scenario, schools can avoid the unseemly annual local spectacle of competing with parks and recreation and the county police for local funding for basic education services.

A Word to Business and Public Leaders

Finally, I want to speak directly to my friends and former colleagues in the business community, and I want to say a word to university leaders and elected public officials as well.

Most great changes begin in fits and starts. The important thing is not how they begin, but that they begin. Once launched, good ideas take on a life of their own.

The school reform movement is a classic case of a great movement moving forward, being halted, and then advancing again. It began in its modern manifestation with publication of *A Nation at Risk* in 1983. The nation's governors took the reins for much of the rest of that decade. President Bush and then President Clinton tried to move reform along by supporting and advancing the national education goals. New American Schools has played a part by underwriting exciting new school models. But the standards-based reform thrust was in danger of losing its momentum in the middle of the 1990s until the business community and the nation's governors got together to announce their continued commitment to standards. Education reform has not always been a stately progression, but it has always been an interesting one.

Today, I sense the movement may be losing energy again. It is up to business, academic, and public leaders to see that does not happen.

To my friends in the private sector, I say: Apart from parents and students, no one has as great a stake in the success of the schools as you do. The quality of your work force depends directly on the quality of their performance. You have a lot to do.

You must be there to be counted on when the road to reform turns rough. Stand behind the national education goals. Defend the development of coherent standards. Forge partnerships with the schools in your local communities. Understand, too, the power you possess to move reform along. You can leave a legacy of learning by recommending the expansion of charter school laws. You should support trials of school choice to help the lowest-income, inner-city children attend private schools. Press for amendments in collective bargaining laws to permit schools to hire teachers directly. Insist on serious evaluations of reform initiatives, including the development of assessments with some teeth in them. And do not be afraid to support the creation of new organizations to provide education in your communities so that truly new kinds of public schools can be developed.

Above all, make sure that prospective employees understand that you want to know not only that they completed high school, but also what they learned while they were there. Your reward will be a more highly skilled work force and stronger, more coherent communities around your plants and offices.

Leaders of the academic world also have a crucial part to play. Your colleges and universities spend billions fixing the learning flaws you find among your entering students. Yet for the most part, your institutions have been notably silent in the reform debate. We have heard little from you on the national education goals, and even less on standards. This disinterest is both surprising and unbecoming. You need to get behind primary and secondary school reform in a major way.

You need to do something else as well. The recent announcement that 60 percent of the candidates for teaching licenses in Massachusetts failed a statewide test for teachers (and that more than one-fourth flunked a basic test of reading and writing) confirms the worst fears of many of us. Too many teacher education programs are academic wastelands. This development in Massachusetts reveals an astonishing state of affairs in teacher education. It is your responsibility, and you must fix it. Although the effort may be painful in the short run, over the long haul you will benefit through better-prepared entering students.

Public officials clearly have a part to do as well. The public's trust in your performance may very well turn on how well you handle the issue of education. Few things are as close to your constituents' hearts. Policymakers at the national level owe the public support for the national education goals and a standards-based reform movement to back them up. Now is no time to squander the policy gains of the last seventeen years.

Public officials at the state level should be thinking about legislation to advance the agenda defined in this book. Governors and state legislators should be crafting legislation to support standards and school autonomy. You should encourage greater flexibility at the local level and more parental choice. You need to demonstrate unflinching commitment to the ideal of a new kind of public school. The forces of inertia are always there to force reformers back to the status quo. You need to hold out the prospect of schools that are better because they offer greater variety and embody basic democratic values.

The standard to which you can repair is creating the conditions at the state and local level that do not simply permit innovations like those supported by New American Schools, but that require them. New American Schools can help provide the supply; you can help create the demand. State laws need to be combed ferociously to root out provisions hampering innovation and to create provisions encouraging greater flexibility and choice at the local level.

At the local level, school boards, newly empowered with state legislation, should turn their attention from personnel issues and micromanaging schools to monitoring how well the superintendent manages the new system or federation of independent schools described here. Your major personnel decision should be hiring the superintendent and holding him or her accountable for system performance. Your reward will be a legacy of learning for your communities.

A Final Word: The Tipping Point and Coming to Scale

In the face of the difficulties facing educational reform, the temptation to lose heart is always present. Why keep trying when you keep getting slapped down? Why not yield the field to the status quo and throw in the towel?

And yet slow as it is, reform is making progress. Tools are in place today—national goals and a new commitment to quality—that were nowhere on the public radar screen a generation ago. And additional tools are under discussion now—new standards, novel forms of assessment, and greater flexibility and choice in the system—that could not be discussed civilly as recently as five years ago. Like fission, reform is hard to get moving, but once it reaches critical mass it sustains itself. Education reform has not reached that point yet, but it would be a mistake to give up. The breakthrough might arrive with startling speed.

Writing in the *New Yorker* in June 1996, Malcolm Gladwell noted that social scientists were beginning to consider the behavior and development of epidemics as an accurate analogy for the behavior, development, and possible resolution of serious social problems.[10] People who study epidemics worry about what they call the "tipping point," Gladwell reported. Above this point, an ordinary phenomenon such as the twenty-four-hour flu can start raging out of control. Below it, the incidence of infection can take a nose dive. Every epidemic, according to the epidemiologists, has its "tipping point"; a relatively small change that occurs near that point can have a startling effect up or down.

How does the tipping point theory apply to school reform and more broadly to social policy? In short, it helps explain why people can work and work and work and get almost no payoff for their efforts if they have not approached the threshold of the tipping point. At the same time, it also means that one more modest effort might provoke a dramatic response.

Tipping-point theory explains the success of the cleanup of the New York City Transit Authority in the early 1990s, Gladwell said. The transit authority was convinced that seemingly trivial problems such as graffiti on the cars and people jumping over turnstiles were important because they invited more serious crimes. By attacking these relatively minor transgressions, the transit authority also succeeded in lowering the incidence of theft and assault. Something similar appears to have happened with New York crime. Citywide, the violent crime rate dropped like a stone in the 1990s. It all began when the city stopped tolerating petty harassment such as "squeegee men" on the street. The strategy appeared to work, both in the subways and on the streets, reports Gladwell. Without knowing where it was, the city reached its "tipping point" in both areas.

Consider the problems the ground rules above are designed to address: parents who expect the schools to do their job for them; schools that insist on assigning children to neighborhood schools; tolerance for shoddy performance and low expectations; lack of accountability; student assessment without consequences; and patently unfair funding patterns. We need hardly look any further for the tipping points required to bring school reform to scale. The ground rules outlined here are designed to correct these obvious failures. When they do, the reform momentum they have created will soon become unstoppable.

The late Ben Edlund, former superintendent in Moses Lake, Washington, understood this. When parents and citizens begin to feel they own their schools again, he promised, "the results will be a wonder to behold."

ACHIEVING THE NATIONAL EDUCATION GOALS:

Nine Keys to Systemic Reform

1. Mission and Values. Define the basic beliefs, commitments, and values that will allow American schools and their students to achieve what they need to achieve.

2. High Expectations. Create a climate in which educators, parents, and citizens understand that all children can learn and all of them can achieve at very high and demanding levels.

3. Standards. Define crisply and in measurable terms what students must know and be able to do to function effectively as adults in the family, the workplace and the community.

4. Assessment. Use assessment strategies that are rich enough to measure whether students are able to meet the standards defined under principle 3.

5. Accountability. Design and implement an accountability system that provides for positive and negative consequences for school teams and the central office (including the superintendent) that are rooted in student performance.

6. Teacher Training. Design and implement an intensive and sustained system of professional development.

Derived from the Business Roundtable's "Nine Essential Components of Reform."

7. Preschool Programs. Assure a quality, developmentally appropriate prekindergarten program for all children.

8. Out-of-School Needs. Work with other agencies, public and private, to meet the health and social service needs of children that are barriers to learning.

9. Technology. Use technology to improve instruction and to manage information in innovative ways.

Defining the Terms of the Standards Debate

CONFUSED ABOUT STANDARDS AND ASSESSMENTS? You are not alone. Here are definitions of the key terms, using a standard of physical fitness, developed by standards experts to clarify the terms of the debate. The definitions come directly from Denis P. Doyle and Susan Pimentel, *Raising the Standard: An Eight-Step Action Guide for Schools and Communities* (Thousand Oaks, Calif.: Corwin Press, 1997).

1. Goal: Students are physically fit.

A goal is the end result of a learning experience. A goal is often not measurable in an immediate sense. It reflects a state of being rather than a state of action. A goal reflects a purpose for instruction but does not designate the specific abilities that the learner will possess.

2. Content (or exit) standards: Twelve-year-old students are able to run one mile. (A standard benchmarked to the President's Council on Physical Fitness.)

A content standard supports the goal. It defines what students must know and be able to do—the knowledge and skills essential to meeting the goal. . . . A content standard . . . is brief, crisp and to the point. It is written in jargon-free English so parents, teachers, and children can understand it. . . .

3. Performance objectives: Twelve-year-old students understand the physiology of muscles, bones, and the cardiovascular system; they are able to warm up and cool down safely; and they are able to pace themselves and breathe correctly while running.

Performance objectives contain all the skills and knowledge a person needs to master the content standard. They detail the content standards.

4. Performance standards: Twelve-year-old boys are able to run one mile in 7 minutes, 11 seconds; twelve-year-old girls, in 8 minutes, 23 seconds.

Performance standards say how good is good enough to meet the content standard. They indicate how competent or adept a student demonstration must be to show attainment of the content standard. Without performance standards, a deliberate, unhurried stroll could constitute running a mile. Performance standards indicate the quality of student performance—is it acceptable, excellent, or somewhere in between? Some districts also include the nature of the evidence (such as an essay, a mathematical proof, a scientific experiment or, in the case of physical fitness, running a mile) required to demonstrate that the content standard has been met.

5. Assessments or tests: Twelve-year-old students run one mile, demonstrating their ability to use proper form, and take a written test, demonstrating their understanding of the physiology of running.

Tests measure students' ability to meet the performance standard. Again, the performance standard specifies the student's degree of proficiency, defining what it means to run the mile in expert, advanced, competent, or less-than-competent fashion.

6. Curriculum Frameworks: These set out units on physiology, questions, and topics to cover; suggested reading material; and training sessions needed to help twelve-year-olds run one mile.

Curriculum frameworks are best characterized as descriptions of what should take place in the classroom; they flesh out in greater detail the topics, themes, units, and questions contained within standards. They are guides for teachers that address instructional techniques, recommended activities, and modes of presentation. . . . Unlike standards, curricula can vary—from state to state, city to city, even school to school—provided they focus on delivering the "big" ideas and concepts [underlying] a set of standards. . . .

Resources for Change

THE FOLLOWING WRITTEN MATERIALS and organizations are good resources not only for following up points raised in this book but in marshaling arguments in favor of school reform.

Written Materials

Each of the issues associated with school reform has entire libraries devoted to it. Here, by major area, are the handful of key resources you need to make the case for change.

The Education Crisis

Jeanne Allen and Angela Dale, *The School Reform Handbook: How to Improve Your Schools* (Washington: Center for Education Reform, 1995).

> An acerbic handbook about the education reform movement, it takes on the "the blob" of the education establishment, school waste, unions, school administrators and boards, and the U.S. Department of Education. Provides useful information on who is in charge, how to make your voice heard, and how to work with the local political and media structure to promote change.

Center on National Education Policy, *Do We Still Need Public Schools?* (Washington: 1996).

> This brief volume, which could not be more different from the Allen-Dale handbook, examines the purpose of public schools in a democracy and the nature of the current school crisis and suggests the need for a public conversation about the shape and future of our schools.

Louis V. Gerstner, Jr., and others, *Reinventing Education: Entrepreneurship in America's Public Schools* (Dutton, 1994).

> Lou Gerstner, chairman and CEO of IBM, and his coauthors present a powerful statement on the importance of education to American society and lay out a reform roadmap emphasizing goals, leadership, teacher development, high expectations for students, and the kinds and level of support required of parents and community leaders.

National Center for Education Statistics, *Pursuing Excellence: A Study of U.S. Twelfth-Grade Mathematics and Science Achievement in International Context.* NCES 98-049 (U.S. Department of Education, 1998).

> This volume contains the basic data to debunk the myth that everything is just fine. Here you find how typical students (as well as the nation's best) shape up in international comparisons. The picture is not encouraging.

National Commission on Excellence in Education, *A Nation at Risk: The Imperative for Educational Reform* (Washington: 1983).

> Published in 1983, this report launched the reform movement that endures to this day. Some of the data are dated, but the point of view remains fresh. The report remains the classic statement of the importance of schools to the American future.

Nature of Schools Today

Gerald Grant, *The World We Created at Hamilton High* (Harvard University Press, 1988).

> A beautifully written, well researched, evocative picture of the contemporary urban high school. Grant's book moves the debate about schooling beyond policy and slogans to a real building, and real students and teachers, in a community with a very real and complicated history.

John I. Goodlad, *A Place Called School: Prospects for the Future* (McGraw-Hill, 1984).

> This book is one of the most detailed examinations ever completed of American schools. Based on years the author and his colleagues spent in schools across the country, it is a gold mine of information about students, teachers, school administration, and community support.

Tracy Kidder, *Among Schoolchildren* (Avon Books, 1989).

> A national bestseller, this is another elegant book about a real school, written by a Pulitzer Prize–winning author who spent a year in a fifth-grade classroom in the depressed "Flats" of Holyoke, Massachusetts, watching the struggles and small triumphs of a teacher and her class.

Diane Ravitch, *The Troubled Crusade: American Education, 1945–1980* (Basic Books, 1983).

> Ravitch is one of our most lucid thinkers and thoughtful writers about education policy and history. This tour de force chronicles the puzzling developments in American education in the years following World War II. Essential to understanding the schools we have today.

Kenneth Shore, *The Parents' Public School Handbook* (Simon and Schuster, 1994).

> If you want to work with today's schools, this book tells you how to do it. This handbook is packed with information explaining how the schools work, who does what, how to make your voice heard, and how to work with your children's teachers and help your children get a good start.

Expectations and Standards

Denis P. Doyle and Susan Pimentel, *Raising the Standard: An Eight-Step Action Guide for Schools and Communities* (Thousand Oaks, Calif.: Corwin Press, Inc., 1997).

> If you are not satisfied with the current schools, this book describes how to change them. As a practical matter, it is the only book about standards that citizens and local educators need. It is an action agenda that covers the entire topic in crisp, clear, easy-to-read prose, remarkably free of most education jargon. It includes down-to-earth advice on how to proceed and is accompanied by a CD-ROM—an "electronic book," that provides much greater detail, for interested readers.

Diane Ravitch, *National Standards in American Education: A Citizens Guide* (Brookings, 1995).

This book is the policy accompaniment to the Doyle-Pimentel volume. It has a very simple message: If clear and consistent goals for learning can be set for all American children—the rich and the poor, the gifted and the ordinary—then all of these children will be better educated than they are likely to be now. Lays out the educational, historical, political, and social issues associated with standards.

Straightening Out the System

Susan H. Fuhrman, ed., *Designing Coherent Education Policy: Improving the System* (San Francisco: Jossey-Bass, 1993).

Useful compendium of articles and policy prescriptions by leading advocates of "systemic" reform. Contents range from early childhood care and academic standards to politics of coherence and need to "align" system components.

Marshall S. Smith and others, "State Policy and Systemic School Reform," *Educational Technology* 32 (November 1992): 31–36.

One of the seminal pieces on "systemic" reform, this article argues for a supportive state policy structure for sustained school-level reform, including a unified vision and goals, a coherent instructional guidance system aligning curriculum, materials, and professional development, and a restructured governance system.

Hard-Wiring Innovation into the System

John E. Chubb and Terry M. Moe, *Politics, Markets, and America's Schools* (Brookings, 1990).

The authors' thesis that market-like mechanisms, such as vouchers and school choice, needed to be introduced to public education created a sensation among educators when it appeared a decade ago.

Chester E. Finn, Jr., Bruno V. Manno, and Louann Bierlein, *Charter Schools in Action: What Have We Learned?* (Indianapolis: Hudson Institute, 1996).

A comprehensive examination of forty-three charter schools in seven states, involving about six hundred interviews with teachers, parents, students, and school administrators and more than one hundred interviews with state officials. Indispensable to anyone who wants to understand the charter-school movement and its energy.

Edward B. Fiske, *Smart Schools, Smart Kids: Why Do Some Schools Work?* (New York: Touchstone Books, 1992).

The long-time education writer for the *New York Times,* "Ted" Fiske, reveals the results of his travels across the country examining innovation in American schools and draws lessons from his experience.

Charles L. Glenn, *Choice of Schools in Six Nations* (U.S. Department of Education, 1989).

There may be others, but this is the only book we know of that describes public systems of school choice in an international context. It suggests that "public education" can be thought of in quite different ways from the manner in which most Americans understand it.

Paul T. Hill, Lawrence C. Pierce, and James W. Guthrie, *Reinventing Public Education: How Contracting Can Transform America's Schools* (University of Chicago Press, 1997).

The authors argue that a widespread system of charter-like contracts would radically improve public education. Their thesis is that requiring school boards and superintendents to manage schools under formal contracts with private providers—contracts specifying the type and quality of instruction expected—would permit superintendents and boards to concentrate on improving student performance.

New American Schools, *Blueprints for School Success: A Guide to New American Schools Designs* (Arlington, Va.: Educational Research Service, 1998).

Well-written overview of New American Schools, describing the basic principles guiding all of its design teams, the ways that schools and districts can work with the teams, and interesting, detailed descriptions of each of the eight teams.

Olatokunbo S. Fasholo and Robert E. Slavin, "Schoolwide Reform Models: What Works?" *Phi Delta Kappan* (January 1998): 370–79.

This article provides a very useful review of some of the major schoolwide reform models, including assessments of the evidence about their effectiveness.

Organizations Active in the Reform Movement

Accelerated Schools
Stanford University, CERAS 109
Stanford, CA 94305-3084
415-725-7158

> Developed the "accelerated schools" program described in chapter 8, a program designed to boost achievement of low-income elementary school students by accelerating their learning.

ACHIEVE
1280 Massachusetts Avenue, Suite 410
Cambridge, MA 02138
617-496-6300

> Created by the nation's governors and business leaders in 1996 to advance standards and evaluate assessment systems.

America's Choice Design Network
700 11th Street, NW, Suite 750
Washington, DC 20001
202-783-3668

> Formerly the National Alliance for Restructuring Education, this New American Schools team has developed a comprehensive design for kindergarten through grade twelve to implement state-of-the-art performance standards and assessments, highly innovative curriculum materials, community engagement processes, and innovative school leadership and management practices.

ATLAS Communities
Educational Development Center
55 Chapel Street
Newton, MA 02160
617-969-7100

> One of eight NAS teams, ATLAS Communities (Authentic Teaching, Learning, and Assessment for all Students) is a partnership of the Coalition of Essential Schools (Brown), the School Development Program (Yale), Project Zero (Harvard), and the Educational Development Center. Its emphases are on improving learning for all students, evaluating students through a variety of assessment tools, professional devel-

opment of teachers, involving families and communities, and reorganizing the internal structures and decisionmaking processes in schools and districts.

Business Roundtable
1615 L Street, NW, Suite 1100
Washington, DC 20036
202-872-1260

In response to President George Bush's 1989 challenge urging business leaders to make a personal commitment to improve American schools, the BRT developed a CEO-led effort to promote standards-based reform in every state.

Coalition of Essential Schools
Box 1938
Brown University
Providence, RI 02912
401-863-3384

An organization of more than nine hundred secondary schools (public and private, urban, suburban, and rural) attempting to change themselves along the lines of nine essential "Common Principles" developed by coalition founder Theodore R. Sizer in 1984. The principles emphasize such things as helping adolescents use their minds well, maintaining simple school goals, applying the goals to all students, personalizing education as much as possible, and employing the practical metaphor of the student-as-worker (not the teacher-as-deliverer-of-instructional-services).

Co-NECT Schools
Bolt, Beranek, and Newman
150 Cambridge Park Drive
Cambridge, MA 02138
617-873-3081

A New American Schools' design team with an innovative approach to helping educators use technology for comprehensive school change. The design stresses high expectations and schoolwide accountability from kindergarten through grade twelve, learning by doing, assessments of school and student performance, small learning communities, and sensible use of the best technology available.

Core Knowledge Foundation
2012-B Morton Drive
Charlottesville, VA 22903
804-977-7550
> Advances the concepts of E. D. Hirsch, Jr. by providing a set of curriculum ideas to communities, citizens, and schools interested in a rigorous common core of learning.

Council for Basic Education
1319 F Street, NW, Suite 900
Washington, DC 20004
202-347-4171
> Washington-based group advocating common, traditional curriculum for all students.

The Education Trust
1725 K Street, NW, Suite 200
Washington, DC 20006
202-293-1217
> Washington-based group advocating high standards and attention to the needs of both low-income and minority students in the school-reform process.

Expeditionary Learning
122 Mount Auburn Street
Cambridge, MA 02138
617-576-1260
> A comprehensive NAS design for kindergarten through grade twelve based on principles growing out of the Outward Bound movement. Stresses that most people learn things better by doing than by listening to people talk about them, and that qualities of character and community are at least as important to nourish and teach as academic skills and knowledge. Students spend most of each school day in purposeful, rigorous, "learning expeditions"—in-depth studies of a single topic, generally lasting six to twelve weeks.

Modern Red Schoolhouse
Hudson Institute
5395 Emerson Way
Indianapolis, IN 46226
317-545-1000

> The Modern Red Schoolhouse is designed to take the principles and virtues of the little red schoolhouse (which did not work well for all) and make them work in today's diverse, complex society. An NAS design team, the Modern Red Schoolhouse takes the expectations for achievement and community support embodied in its predecessor and infuses them with technological and informational resources.

National Board for Professional Teaching Standards
26555 Evergreen Road, Suite 400
Southfield, MI 48076
800-229-9074

> A complex and evolving experiment to improve the quality of teaching in the United States by developing Master Teachers, teachers certified at the highest levels of competence in subject-matter knowledge and pedagogical skills and compensated accordingly.

New American Schools
1000 Wilson Boulevard, Suite 2710
Arlington, VA 22209
703-908-9500

> A nonpartisan, nonprofit organization founded in 1991 by business leaders who wanted to improve the quality of public education in the United States. Driven by the mission of helping large numbers of schools help large numbers of students achieve at high levels, NAS has underwritten the development of eight design team concepts (including one year of development and two years of field testing) and since 1994 has helped the design teams begin to scale up nationally. By 1998 New American Schools' designs were being implemented in about 1,500 schools enrolling 350,000 students.

Purpose-Centered Education
345 Hudson Street
New York, NY 10014
212-989-2002

Another NAS team, formerly known as the Audrey Cohen College, this design for grades kindergarten through grade twelve focuses all student learning—from math and science to English and social studies—on a complex, meaningful, overarching "purpose" that contributes to the world at large. The aim is to help students become eager, confident learners through twenty-four developmentally appropriate purposes such as "We Work for Safety" (first grade), "We Work for Good Health" (fourth grade), "I Take Charge of My Learning" (seventh grade), and "I Use Science and Technology to Help Shape a Just and Productive Society" (tenth grade).

Roots and Wings
Johns Hopkins University
3505 North Charles Street
Baltimore, MD 21218
800-548-4998

An NAS team started from the foundation laid by the Success for All program (see below), Roots and Wings is centered on a guarantee: Every child will progress successfully through the elementary grades, no matter what it takes.

School Development Program
Ed Joyner Child Study Center
230 South Frontage Rd., P.O. Box 20790
New Haven, CT 06520-7900
203-785-2548

A comprehensive approach to reform in elementary and middle schools, this program emphasizes partnerships between the school and community. Building the program around three teams—school planning and management, mental health, and parents—the aim is to have the teams work together to create comprehensive plans for school reform.

Success for All
Johns Hopkins University
3505 North Charles Street
Baltimore, MD 21218
800-548-4998

A program to provide elementary schools serving large numbers of at-risk students with innovative curricula and instructional methods in reading, writing, and language arts. (With the addition of programs in mathematics, social studies, and science, Success for All became the Roots and Wings program of New American Schools; see above.) One-to-one tutoring, family support services, intensive professional development and coaching, and assessment are major parts of the Success for All approach.

Urban Learning Centers
315 West 9th Street, Suite 1110
Los Angeles, CA 90115
213-622-5237

Another NAS team, Urban Learning Centers, which has concentrated its efforts in the Los Angeles area, attempts to reorganize schools at all grade levels serving low-income urban students into learning communities, with connections across grades, strong community support, and high levels of participation. The design calls for substantial changes in methods of teaching and learning, management and governance, and the ways schools address the health and well-being of students.

Notes

Introduction

1. Lamar Alexander, "America 2000: An Education Strategy," *The Commonwealth* (a publication of the Commonwealth Club of California, San Francisco), October 2, 1992.

2. Insightful recollections from participants in the Bush administration's education legislative program can be found in John F. Jennings, ed., *National Issues in Education: The Past is Prologue* (Bloomington, Ind., and Washington, D.C.: Phi Delta Kappa International and Institute for Educational Leadership, 1993). Similar tales from the first Clinton term can be found in John F. Jennings, ed., *National Issues in Education: Elementary and Secondary Education Act* (Bloomington, Ind., and Washington, D.C.: Phi Delta Kappa International and Institute for Educational Leadership, 1995).

3. New American Schools Development Corporation, "Designs for a New Generation of American Schools: Request for Proposals" (Arlington, Va.: October 1991).

4. Author interview with John Anderson, president of New American Schools, January 29, 1997.

Chapter One

1. Each of these startling numbers is based on well-regarded academic or official sources. Date on dropouts are notoriously fickle, depending on who is counted and at what age. The federal government's National Center for Education Statistics (NCES) reported that 24.8 percent of Americans aged twenty-five and over did not have a high school diploma in 1990 (the source of the 25 percent figure cited in the text) and that in 1996, 11.1 percent of those aged sixteen to twenty-four were high school dropouts. The latter figure is actually a surprisingly high number considering that it includes sixteen-, seventeen-, and eighteen-year-olds, most of whom, in this day and age, would be expected to be in school. See National Center for Education Statistics, *Digest of Education Statistics* (Washington, D.C.: 1997), tables 11, 102.

According to data from the Massachusetts Department of Education, in April 1998 only 41 percent of all first-time candidates passed the Massachusetts Educator Certification Tests. Fully 30 percent failed the reading portion of the tests. "Education Commissioner to Appoint Panel to Review the Massachusetts Educator Certification Tests," press release, Massachusetts Department of Education, July 27, 1999; see also, Massachusetts Department of Education, *Massachusetts Educator Certification Tests: Technical Report Summary* (1999). The Lake Wobegon phenomenon was identified by RAND Corporation researcher, Daniel Koretz, among others; see Daniel Koretz, "Arriving in Lake Wobegon: Are Standardized Tests Exaggerating Achievement and Distorting Instruction?" *American Educator* 12 (Summer, 1988): 8–15. The international spending and achievement comparisons were developed by the international office of the Third International Mathematics and Science Study. And the comparison of high school completion rates is included in Organization for Economic Cooperation and Development, *Education at a Glance: OECD Indicators* (Paris: 1998), table C2.3. (OECD, incidentally, puts the U.S. high school graduation rate at 72 percent, yet a different figure from the two published by NCES.)

2. Harold W. Stevenson and James W. Stigler, *The Learning Gap: Why Our Schools Are Failing and What We Can Learn from Japanese and Chinese Education* (New York: Simon and Schuster, 1992).

3. Author interview with S. Jefferson Kennard III, December 10, 1996.

4. Author interview with Edward Bales, April 25, 1997.

5. For a discussion of the development of the length of the school year since the nineteenth century, see National Education Commission on Time and Learning, *Prisoners of Time: Schools and Programs Making Time Work for Students and Teachers* (Washington, D.C.: 1994). Originally pegged at about 60 days annually to permit the children of farmers and ranchers to help out at home, school calen-

dars have slowly increased to about 180 days in most states, compared with the 210- to 220-day school year common in much of Europe and Asia.

6. Author interview with Roy Romer, February 1998.

7. See, for example, Peter Drucker, "Toward a Knowledge-Based Society," *Current* (February 1993):4; and Drucker, "Beyond the Information Revolution, *Atlantic Monthly* (October 1999):14.

8. See, for example, National Center for Education Statistics, *The Condition of Education, 1997* (U.S. Department of Education, 1998), table 23-1, which indicates that the United States is first among twenty-two nations in the proportion of adults with a bachelor's degree (24.4 percent).

9. David W. Breneman, "Remediation in Higher Education: Its Extent and Cost," in *Brookings Papers on Education Policy,* edited by Diane Ravitch (Brookings, 1998).

10. Ibid.

11. Kevin Phillips, *The Politics of Rich and Poor: Wealth and the American Electorate* (New York: Random House, 1990).

12. U.S. Department of Commerce, *Statistical Abstract of the United States, 1996* (Washington, D.C.: 1996), tables 91, 92.

13. Harold L. Hodgkinson, "Remarks to the Inaugural Meeting of the Missouri Superintendents Forum," Kansas City, Missouri, October 17, 1997. (Unpublished manuscript available from Kauffman Foundation, Kansas City.)

14. Ibid.

15. Ibid.

16. Ibid.

17. U.S. Department of Commerce, *Statistical Abstract of the United States, 1996*, table 624.

18. Gerald F. Seib, "The Real Issue: Can Americans Hang Together?" *Wall Street Journal,* October 25, 1996, p. A16.

19. The reading assessment was administered in 1991, reported in 1993, and reissued by the U.S. Department of Education in 1996. See National Center for Education Statistics, *Reading Literacy in the United States,* NCES 96-258 (U.S. Department of Education, 1996).

Chapter Two

1. National Commission on Excellence in Education, *A Nation at Risk: The Imperative for Educational Reform* (U.S. Department of Education, April 1983).

2. Ibid., 8.

3. Ibid, 8–9.

4. See for example, David C. Berliner and Bruce J. Biddle, *The Manufactured Crisis: Myths, Fraud, and the Attack on America's Public Schools* (Reading, Mass.: Addison-Wesley Publishing, 1995); David W. Grissmer and others, *Student Achievement and the Changing American Family* (Santa Monica, Calif.: RAND Corporation, 1994); and Gerald W. Bracey, "TIMSS, Rhymes with 'Dims,' as in 'Witted,'" *Phi Delta Kappan* 79 (May 1998): 686.

5. David Tyack and Larry Cuban, *Tinkering toward Utopia, A Century of Public School Reform* (Harvard University Press, 1995). In asking the question posed by Tyack and Cuban, and using their data throughout this document, the authors in no way want to imply that Tyack and Cuban agree with the authors' conclusions. In fact, both Tyack and Cuban clearly believe that criticisms of American schools have been overstated.

6. National Center for Educational Statistics, *High School Students Ten Years after "A Nation at Risk,"* NCES 95-764 (U.S. Department of Education, 1995).

7. Author interview with Milton Goldberg, March 4, 1997.

8. National Center for Educational Statistics, *NAEP 1994 Trends in Academic Progress,* NCES 97-095 (U.S. Department of Education, 1996), iv.

9. National Center for Education Statistics, *Reading Literacy in the United States.*

10. See National Center for Educational Statistics, *Pursuing Excellence: A Study of U.S. Eighth-Grade Mathematics and Science Teaching, Learning, Curriculum, and Achievement,* NCES 97-198 (U.S. Department of Education, 1996); National Center for Educational Statistics, *Pursuing Excellence: A Study of U.S. Fourth-Grade Mathematics and Science Achievement in International Context,* NCES 97-255 (U.S. Department of Education, 1997); and National Center for Educational Statistics, *Pursuing Excellence: A Study of U.S. Twelfth-Grade Mathematics and Science Achievement in International Context,* NCES 98-049 (U.S. Department of Education, 1998).

11. Robert Greene, "Poor in Science," Associated Press report, February 24, 1998.

12. National Center for Educational Statistics, *Pursuing Excellence: A Study of U.S. Eighth Grade Mathematics and Science,* 25.

13. Organization for Economic Cooperation and Development, *Education at a Glance: OECD Indicators, 1998* (Paris: 1998), table C2.3.

Chapter Three

1. Secretary's Commission on Achieving Necessary Skills (SCANS Commission), *What Work Requires of Schools* (U.S. Department of Labor, 1991);

and SCANS Commission, *Learning a Living* (U.S. Department of Labor, 1992).

2. Until the 1950s schools in the South were legally segregated, and de facto segregation continued, North and South, long after the U.S. Supreme Court's decision in 1954 declaring desegregation unconstitutional. African American students were not the only ones to suffer; most public school systems refused to educate children with disabilities well into the 1970s.

3. Diane Ravitch, correspondence with authors, June 22, 1998.

4. Joel Spring, *The American School, 1642–1996,* 4th ed. (McGraw-Hill, 1997), 9.

5. Ibid., 16.

6. Ravitch, correspondence with authors.

7. David Tyack and Larry Cuban, *Tinkering toward Utopia, A Century of Public School Reform* (Harvard University Press, 1995), 16.

8. National Center for Education Statistics, *Digest of Education Statistics, 1996* (U.S. Department of Education, 1997), table 8.

9. The National Education Association at the time was a professional organization, not a union. In fact, NEA explicitly rejected unionism as an activity until pressures of various kinds (from members, new teachers, and a newly militant American Federation of Teachers) encouraged it to move in that direction in the 1960s and 1970s.

10. Diane Ravitch, *The Troubled Crusade: American Education, 1945–1980* (Basic Books, 1983), 48.

11. Ibid., 55.

12. Author interview with Paul T. Hill, March 17, 1999.

13. Paul T. Hill, Gail E. Foster, and Tamar Gendler, *High Schools with Character* (Santa Monica, Calif.: RAND Corporation, 1990).

14. Classes are no longer "cut" but "ditched." 1990s students now speak casually of "ditching" class periods, school days, even entire school years, as in "basically I ditched sophomore year."

15. National Center for Education Statistics, *Digest of Education Statistics, 1997* (U.S. Department of Education, 1998), table 88.

16. Ibid., table 38.

17. Ibid., table 39.

18. While at the National Institute of Education, Doyle helped to finance a volume on the effects of rural school consolidation: Jonathan P. Sher, ed., *Education in Rural America: A Reassessment of Conventional Wisdom* (Boulder, Colo.: Westview Press, 1977).

19. Tyack and Cuban, *Tinkering toward Utopia,* 17.

20. Ibid, 16.

21. National Center for Education Statistics, *Digest of Education Statistics, 1996,* table 94.

22. Arthur Powell, Eleanor Farrar, and David K. Cohen, *The Shopping Mall High School: Winners and Losers in the Educational Marketplace* (Houghton Mifflin, 1985).

23. Gerald Grant, *The World We Created at Hamilton High* (Harvard University Press, 1988).

24. Tyack and Cuban, *Tinkering toward Utopia,* p. 48.

Chapter Four

1. Author interview with Howard Fuller, July 8, 1998.

2. See, for example, Ron Sunseri, *Outcome-Based Education; Understanding the Truth about Education Reform* (Sisters, Ore.: Multnomah Books, 1994).

3. Author interview, Susan Traiman, director of Education Reform, Business Roundtable, April 12, 1997.

4. Author interview, William Raspberry, June 8, 1997.

5. Albert Shanker, "Restructuring American Education," in *Proceedings: Roundtable on Urban Education* (Washington, D.C.: American Council on Education, 1989).

6. Arthur E. Wise, *Legislated Learning: The Bureaucratization of the American Classroom* (University of California Press, 1979).

7. Paul T. Hill, *Reinventing Public Education* (Santa Monica, Calif.: RAND Corporation, 1995).

8. National Commission on Teaching and America's Future, *What Matters Most: Teaching for America's Future* (New York: September 1996).

9. Carnegie units were an invention of the Carnegie Foundation for the Advancement of Teaching early in the twentieth century, and they are still in use. As late as 1900 hard and fast distinctions between secondary and collegiate work were often hard to make. In an effort to improve the situation, the Carnegie Foundation defined acceptable precollegiate preparation as consisting of so many years instruction in English, mathematics, science, social studies, and foreign language. To make sure that the "years" were consistent, each subject-year was defined in terms of Carnegie units, normally requiring 150 or more hours of instruction.

10. David Tyack and Larry Cuban, *Tinkering toward Utopia: A Century of Public School Reform* (Harvard University Press, 1995).

11. Public Agenda Foundation, *Divided Within, Besieged Without* (New York: 1993).

12. Ibid.

13. Owen "Brad" Butler, "Foundation for Hope," in *Proceedings: Round-table on Urban Education* (Washington, D.C.: American Council on Education, 1989).

Chapter Five

1. Paul Ingrassia and Joseph B. White, *Comeback: The Fall and Rise of the American Automobile Industry* (Simon and Schuster Touchstone Books, 1995), 126–28.

2. Ibid., 127.

3. Author interview with Donald E. Petersen, April 14, 1997.

4. Ibid.

5. Ibid.

6. Ingrassia and White, *Comeback,* 137.

7. Ingrassia and White's invaluable book about the Detroit turnaround, *Comeback,* provides a detailed inside look at the people and the corporate politics behind the products and the profits of Detroit's Big Three.

8. A fascinating account of how the U.S. Army turned this situation around can be found in Paula Span, "Sell All You Can Sell," *Washington Post Magazine,* March 22, 1992, p. 15.

9. Petersen interview.

10. Ibid.

11. Author interview with Edward Bales, April 25, 1997.

12. Bales and Robert Galvin recall that in 1936 Paul Galvin took Bob on a trip to Europe, including an extensive visit to Germany. Convinced that the autobahns going up throughout the Reich were designed to move troops, not just civilians, the senior Galvin returned to the United States to warn that war in Europe was on its way. He thought two-way radio communication might play a part in such a war. At the time, such a radio did not exist. American policemen in their cars, for example, listened to the lower bands on the AM dial to get dispatchers' reports of crimes. Then they had to go to a call box to communicate with the precinct. The senior Galvin turned Galvin Manufacturing successfully to the task of inventing two-way police radios, initially using FM frequencies. Galvin Manufacturing was officially renamed Motorola in 1948.

13. Bales interview.

14. Author interview with Robert Galvin, April 10, 1997.

15. Author interview with Gene Wise, July 20, 1988.

16. Galvin interview.

17. Ibid.

18. Petersen interview.

19. As Ingrassia and White describe in *Comeback,* pp. 90–92, it is crucial that the connecting rods in each engine be the same weight at the top and bottom so the engine runs smoothly. Honda produced smoother, lighter, and shorter connecting rods, each of the same weight, by manufacturing four at a time and keeping them together until they reached the engine. GM produced thousands at a time and dumped them in bins where assembly-line workers had to find four that matched or grind them down until they balanced properly. As a consequence GM cars needed bigger pistons, more piston rings, bigger engine blocks and engines, and a larger engine compartment with a higher hood, to hold an engine with less power—all this extra work, weight, material, and inefficiency simply because four matched rods could not be delivered to the factory floor.

20. See, for example, William H. Davidow and Michael S. Malone, *The Virtual Corporation: Lessons from the World's Most Advanced Companies* (Harper Business, 1992); Southern Technology Council, Southern Growth Policies Board, *Turning to Technology: A Strategic Plan for the Nineties* (Research Triangle, N.C.: 1990); and Business–Higher Education Forum, *Higher Education and Work Readiness: The View from the Corporation* (Washington, D.C.: September 1995).

21. Bales interview.

Chapter Six

1. Two-hundred and sixteen school districts in the United States (about 1.5 percent of all districts) have enrollments exceeding 25,000 students, according to data from the National Center for Education Statistics. Their combined enrollment accounts for 30.5 percent of all students.

2. Author interview with Saul Yanofsky, superintendent, White Plains, New York, April 10, 1997.

3. Albert Shanker, "Restructuring American Education," in *Proceedings: Roundtable on Urban Education* (Washington, D.C.: American Council on Education, 1989).

4. Author interview with Donald E. Petersen, April 14, 1997.

5. The Todd Protectographic Machine was still in use in some small companies as late as the 1970s. It was a device invented by my mother's father, an able and ingenious inventor. The machine protected against financial fraud by embossing the dollar amount on a check so that it could not be altered.

6. John Immerwahr, Jean Johnson, and Adam Kernan-Schloss, *Cross Talk: The Public, the Experts, and Competitiveness* (New York: Public Agenda Foundation and Business–Higher Education Forum, 1991).

7. Jean Johnson, Steve Farkas, and Ali Bers, *Getting By: What American Teenagers Really Think about Their Schools* (New York: Public Agenda Foundation, 1997).

8. Author interview with Ben Canada, November 20, 1998.

9. See for example, Paul T. Hill, Gail E. Foster, and Tamar Gendler, *High Schools with Character* (Santa Monica, Calif.: RAND Corporation, 1990).

Chapter Seven

1. New American Schools Development Corporation, *Designs for a New Generation of American Schools, Request for Proposals* (Arlington, Va.: October 1991).

2. For another interesting example of how Washington insiders look at money, see Diane Ravitch, "Launching a Revolution in Standards and Assessments," *Phi Delta Kappan* (June 1993): 767–72. Although Ravitch thought one of the most important line items in her budget was $5 million for research on student assessment, one senator told her not to waste his time with such small requests. Despite the small request, Congress refused to vote the money.

3. Richard Riley, "Goals 2000: Providing a World-Class Education for Every Child," in *National Issues in Education: Elementary and Secondary Education Act,* edited by John F. Jennings (Bloomington, Ind., and Washington, D.C.: Phi Delta Kappa International and Institute for Educational Leadership, 1995).

4. Educational Research Service, *Blueprints for School Success: A Guide to New American Schools Designs* (Arlington, Va.: n.d.).

5. New American Schools, *Working Toward Excellence: Examining the Effectiveness of New American Schools Designs* (Arlington, Va.: February 1999).

6. Ibid.

7. Lynn Olson, "Memphis Study Tracks Gains in Whole-School Designs," *Education Week,* May 27, 1998, p. 9.

Chapter Eight

1. Author interview with Patricia Garrett, April 24, 1996.

2. National Education Commission on Time and Learning, *Prisoners of Time: Schools and Programs Making Time Work for Students and Teachers* (U.S. Department of Education, September 1994), 30–31.

3. Olatokunbo S. Fashola and Robert Slavin, "Schoolwide Reform Models: What Works?" *Phi Delta Kappan* (January 1998): 374.

4. National Education Commission on Time and Learning, *Prisoners of Time.*

5. Chester E. Finn Jr., Bruno V. Manno, and Louann Bierlein, *Charter Schools in Action: What Have We Learned?* (Indianapolis: Hudson Institute, 1996).

6. Ibid. See also *Massachusetts Department of Education, The Massachusetts Charter School Initiative, 1996 Report* (Boston: 1997).

7. Finn, Manno, and Bierlein, *Charter Schools in Action,* p. 14.

8. Ibid., p. 58.

9. Fashola and Slavin, "Schoolwide Reform Models," 374.

10. Ibid.

11. Danforth Foundation, *Improving Results for Children: Building State and Local Capacity for System Change* (St. Louis: January 1997).

12. Danforth Foundation, *Learnings on Leadership: Highlights of the Meetings of the Forum for the American School Superintendent* (St. Louis: June 1999), 29.

13. Partnership for Kentucky School Reform, *From Dilemma to Opportunity: A Report on Education Reform in Kentucky* (Lexington: February 1996).

14. Danforth Foundation, *Learnings on Leadership,* p. 29.

15. Partnership for Kentucky School Reform, *From Dilemma to Opportunity: A Report on Education Reform in Kentucky 5 Years after the Kentucky Education Reform Act of 1990,* vols. 1 and 2 (Lexington: 1996).

16. Appalachian Education Laboratory, "Education Reform in Rural Kentucky," *Notes from the Field* 6 (September 1998).

17. Governor's Council on Education Reform and Funding, *Putting Children First: Improving Student Performance in Washington State* (Olympia, Wash.: December 1992).

18. Robin J. Lake and others, *Making Standards Work: Active Voices, Focused Learning* (Seattle: University of Washington, Daniel J. Evans School of Public Affairs, Center for Reinventing Public Education, February 1999), 7.

19. Author interview with Robin J. Lake and Paul T. Hill, October 25, 1999.

20. Dick Lilly, "Emphasis on Basics Improves Assessment Scores, Study Shows," *Seattle Times,* February 23, 1999, p. 1.

21. Lake and Hill interview.

Chapter Nine

1. David T. Kearns and Denis P. Doyle, *Winning the Brain Race: A Bold Plan to Make Our Schools Competitive* (San Francisco: ICS Press, 1988).

2. Business–Higher Education Forum, *American Potential: The Human Dimension* (Washington, D.C.: American Council on Education, September 1998).

3. Lowell C. Rose, "Who Cares? And So What?" *Phi Delta Kappan* (June 1998): 722.

4. Daniel Koretz, "Arriving in Lake Wobegon: Are Standardized Tests Exaggerating Achievement and Distorting Instruction?" *American Educator* 12 (Summer 1988): 8–15.

5. Danforth Foundation, *Improving Results for Children: Building State and Local Capacity for System Change* (St. Louis: January 1997).

6. National Commission on Teaching and America's Future, *What Matters Most: Teaching for America's Future* (New York: 1996).

7. Howard L. Fuller, George A. Mitchell, and Michael E. Hartman, *The Milwaukee Public Schools' Teacher Union Contract: Its History, Content, and Impact on Education*, Report 97-1 (Marquette University Institute for the Transformation of Learning, October 1997).

8. The observation that American culture is almost consciously anti-intellectual is so common that it hardly needs support. Historian Richard Hofstadter made it commonplace nearly forty years ago with his ground-breaking book *Anti-Intellectualism in American Life* (Knopf, 1963).

9. John Immerwahr, Jean Johnson, and Adam Kernan-Schloss, *Cross Talk: The Public, The Experts, and Competitiveness* (New York: Public Agenda Foundation and Business–Higher Education Forum, February 1991).

10. Jean Johnson and John Immerwahr, *First Things First: What Americans Expect from the Public Schools* (New York: Public Agenda Foundation, 1994).

11. Author interview with John Immerwahr, September 10, 1998.

12. Gerald Grant, *The World We Created at Hamilton High* (Harvard University Press, 1988).

13. Laurence Steinberg, "Standards Outside the Classroom," in *Brookings Papers on Education Policy, 1998,* edited by Diane Ravitch (Brookings, 1998).

14. For a discussion of these weaknesses, see, for example, Paul T. Hill, Lawrence C. Pierce, and James W. Guthrie, *Reinventing Public Education: How Contracting Can Transform America's Schools* (University of Chicago Press, 1997).

15. Author interview with Ted Sizer, November 26, 1997.

Chapter Ten

1. Author interview with Paul Hill, August 4, 1997.

2. For discussion of these issues, see, for example, Paul T. Hill, Gail E. Foster, and Tamar Gendler, *High Schools with Character* (Santa Monica, Calif., RAND Corporation, 1990). See also several excellent reports from the Public Agenda Foundation, including John Immerwahr, Jean Johnson, and Adam Kernan-Schloss, *Cross Talk: The Public, The Experts, and Competitiveness* (New York: 1991); Jean Johnson and John Immerwahr, *What Americans Expect from Public Schools* (New York: 1994); and Will Friedman, *The Basics:*

Parents Talk about Reading, Writing, Arithmetic, and the Schools (New York, 1995).

3. U.S. Bureau of the Census, *Statistical Abstract of the United States: 1996* (U.S. Department of Commerce, 1996), table 81, p. 65.

4. Ibid.

5. Ibid., table 733, p. 473.

6. Ibid., table 626, p. 400.

7. Ibid., table 347, p. 217.

8. Ibid., table 175, p. 121.

9. Nelda Cambron-McCabe and James Harvey, *Supporting Learning for All Children: A Report on the "Success for All Children" Initiative* (St. Louis: Danforth Foundation, July 1997).

10. Correspondence from Denis P. Doyle to David T. Kearns, June 21, 1999.

11. Ibid.

Chapter Eleven

1. Russian Field Marshall Grigori Potemkin cleaned up many towns and built entire villages of nothing but stage fronts to impress Catherine the Great. When he took her on a tour of the Crimea in 1787 she was reassured that all was well and prosperous in the empire.

2. Paul T. Hill, Lawrence C. Pierce, and James W. Guthrie, *Reinventing Public Education: How Contracting Can Transform America's Schools* (University of Chicago Press, 1997).

3. Several experts have concluded that steep increases in tuition and fees in recent decades are related to the widespread availability of financial aid, particularly subsidized loans. The thinking is that college administrators have justified increasing fees on the theory that needy students can borrow the money. If true, it means that access to student aid has permitted tuition to increase because the aid has expanded the universe of students able to bear the tuition burden. To avoid this potential problem in primary and secondary education, my proposal requires all contractors to accept the public payment as payment in full for students. Nonprofit entities, including independent schools, unwilling to agree to this stipulation would be free to charge what they wish but would not be eligible for public funding. (For a discussion of student aid and its relationship to college tuition, see National Commission on the Cost of Higher Education, *Straight Talk about College Costs and Prices* (Phoenix: Oryx Press, 1998).

4. Charles L. Glenn, *Choice of Schools in Six Nations: France, Netherlands, Belgium, Britain, Canada, West Germany* (U.S. Department of Education, 1989), 49.

5. Education in the United States includes, in addition to 87,000 public schools, about 26,100 private elementary and secondary schools. Of these private schools, 8,300 are Catholic, 12,200 are affiliated with other religious groups, and 5,600 are nonsectarian. See National Center for Education Statistics, *Digest of Education Statistics, 1997,* NCES 98-015 (U.S. Department of Education, 1998), table 59, p.70.

6. Most historians agree that "public schools" in the nineteenth century were hostile to Catholics, that as recently as the 1920s the Ku Klux Klan in Oregon initiated and stood behind anti-Catholic state legislation (which was overturned in the courts) requiring all students to attend public schools, and that Americans United for Separation of Church and State was created after World War II to make sure that pending federal school aid did not include religious schools, particularly Catholic schools. See, for example, Joel Spring, *The American School, 1642–1996,* 4th ed. (McGraw-Hill, 1997), 79–84; and Diane Ravitch, *The Troubled Crusade: American Education, 1945–1980* (Basic Books, 1983), 23–42.

7. The University of Utah provides a comprehensive review of federal and state issues, including separation of church and state, on its website at http://www.reasonmag.com/9701/fe.rick.html. The position of vigorous opponents to any form of public assistance to students in religiously affiliated schools or to the schools themselves is well laid out by the Americans United for Separation of Church and State. The organization's website can be found at http://www.au.org/. A useful and detailed summary of state laws and regulations as they apply to private schools can be found in: L. Patricia Williams, *The Regulation of Private Schools in America: A State-by-State Analysis* (U.S. Department of Education, n.d.). Also available on the Internet at http://oeri2.ed.gov/pubs/RegPrivSchl/title.html.

8. Alisa LaPolt, "Milwaukee Court Decision," Associated Press report, June 10, 1998.

9. Albert Shanker, "Restructuring American Education," in *Proceedings: Roundtable on Urban Education* (Washington, D.C.: American Council on Education, 1989).

10. Glenn, *Choice of Schools in Six Nations,* 214–15.

11. Ibid., 218.

12. David J. Armor and Brett M. Peiser, *Competition in Education: A Case Study of Interdistrict Choice* (Fairfax, Va.: Institute for Public Policy, April 1997).

13. Seymour Fliegel and James MacGuire, *Miracle in East Harlem: The Fight for Choice in Public Education* (New York: Times Books, 1993).

Chapter Twelve

1. See, for example, Madeleine Nash, "How a Child's Brain Develops," *Time*, February 3, 1997, p. 63; and also Education Commission of the States, *Bridging the Gap between Neuroscience and Education* (Denver, September 1996).

2. Danforth Foundation, "Improving Results for Children: Building State and Local Capacity for System Change," highlights of the Policymakers' Program cosponsored by the Danforth Foundation, Education Commission of the States, National Conference of State Legislatures, and the National Governors' Association in San Diego, January 1997. Unpublished manuscript available from the Danforth Foundation, St. Louis.

3. Danforth Foundation, *Learnings on Leadership: Highlights of the Meetings of the Forum for the American School Superintendent* (St. Louis, June 1999), 82.

4. Lowell C. Rose and Alex M. Gallup, "The 30th Annual Phi Delta Kappan/Gallup Poll of the Public's Attitudes toward the Public Schools," *Phi Delta Kappan* 80 (September 1998): 41.

5. Author interview with David Hawkins, December 21, 1998.

6. Author interview with Deborah Meier, April 14, 1997.

7. These standards rely heavily on three sources: the results of NAEP and international literacy assessments and the ensuing consensus that all students should be able to read by the end of third grade and use a newspaper knowledgeably as they enter high school; international analyses of science and mathematics curriculum content conducted as part of the TIMSS assessments and growing support for the idea that the TIMSS international averages are a reasonable benchmark for American performance; and the analyses of school-level standards completed by Denis P. Doyle and Susan Pimentel. See Doyle and Pimentel, *Raising the Standard: An Eight-Step Action Guide for Schools and Communities* (Thousand Oaks, Calif.: Corwin Press, 1997).

8. For a discussion of the relationship between standards, time, and resources, see National Education Commission on Time and Learning, *Prisoners of Time: Schools and Programs Making Time Work for Students and Teachers* (Washington, D.C., 1994).

9. See appendix B for more information about the New Standards Project.

10. Malcolm Gladwell, "The Tipping Point: Why Is the City Suddenly So Much Safer—Could It Be that Crime Really Is an Epidemic?" *New Yorker*, June 3, 1996, p. 32.

Index